# CAMBRIDGE LIBRARY COLLECTION

*Books of enduring scholarly value*

## British and Irish History, Seventeenth and Eighteenth Centuries

The books in this series focus on the British Isles in the early modern period, as interpreted by eighteenth- and nineteenth-century historians, and show the shift to 'scientific' historiography. Several of them are devoted exclusively to the history of Ireland, while others cover topics including economic history, foreign and colonial policy, agriculture and the industrial revolution. There are also works in political thought and social theory, which address subjects such as human rights, the role of women, and criminal justice.

## Diary of John Rous

The diary of John Rous (1584–1644) was edited for the Camden Society in 1856 by Mary Anne Everett Green (1818–95). Rous kept this diary between 1625 and 1643, when he was vicar of Santon Downham in Suffolk, recording both local events and reports of momentous happenings in Britain and abroad from Charles I's accession to the outbreak of the Civil War. M.A.E. Green was educated by her father, a Methodist minister, and began research on historical topics in the British Museum Reading Room and other London archives. She was recommended to Sir John Romilly as an external editor for the Calendar of State Papers project, and was the first to be appointed: her work became the standard which later editors followed. Rous's diary is preceded by an introduction placing its author in his family and historical context, and Green's notes explicate references to the people and events described.

T0371274

Cambridge University Press has long been a pioneer in the reissuing of out-of-print titles from its own backlist, producing digital reprints of books that are still sought after by scholars and students but could not be reprinted economically using traditional technology. The Cambridge Library Collection extends this activity to a wider range of books which are still of importance to researchers and professionals, either for the source material they contain, or as landmarks in the history of their academic discipline.

Drawing from the world-renowned collections in the Cambridge University Library and other partner libraries, and guided by the advice of experts in each subject area, Cambridge University Press is using state-of-the-art scanning machines in its own Printing House to capture the content of each book selected for inclusion. The files are processed to give a consistently clear, crisp image, and the books finished to the high quality standard for which the Press is recognised around the world. The latest print-on-demand technology ensures that the books will remain available indefinitely, and that orders for single or multiple copies can quickly be supplied.

The Cambridge Library Collection brings back to life books of enduring scholarly value (including out-of-copyright works originally issued by other publishers) across a wide range of disciplines in the humanities and social sciences and in science and technology.

# Diary of John Rous

*Incumbent of Santon Downham, Suffolk,
from 1625 to 1642*

Edited by
Mary Anne Everett Green

CAMBRIDGE
UNIVERSITY PRESS

# CAMBRIDGE
## UNIVERSITY PRESS

University Printing House, Cambridge, CB2 8BS, United Kingdom

Cambridge University Press is part of the University of Cambridge.
It furthers the University's mission by disseminating knowledge in the pursuit of
education, learning and research at the highest international levels of excellence.

www.cambridge.org
Information on this title: www.cambridge.org/9781108073882

© in this compilation Cambridge University Press 2014

This edition first published 1856
This digitally printed version 2014

ISBN 978-1-108-07388-2 Paperback

# DIARY OF JOHN ROUS,

INCUMBENT OF

## SANTON DOWNHAM, SUFFOLK,

FROM 1625 TO 1642.

EDITED BY

## MARY ANNE EVERETT GREEN,

AUTHOR OF "LIVES OF THE PRINCESSES OF ENGLAND;" EDITOR OF
"LETTERS OF ROYAL AND ILLUSTRIOUS LADIES."

PRINTED FOR THE CAMDEN SOCIETY.

M.DCCC.LVI.

# COUNCIL OF THE CAMDEN SOCIETY

## FOR THE YEAR 1856-7.

---

*President,*

THE RIGHT HON. LORD BRAYBROOKE, F.S.A.

WILLIAM HENRY BLAAUW, ESQ. M.A., F.S.A.
JOHN BRUCE, ESQ. F.S.A. *Director.*
JOHN PAYNE COLLIER, ESQ. F.S.A. *Treasurer.*
WILLIAM DURRANT COOPER, ESQ. F.S.A.
BOLTON CORNEY, ESQ. M.R.S.L.
JAMES CROSBY, ESQ. F.S.A.
SIR HENRY ELLIS, K.H., F.R.S., Dir.S.A.
THE RIGHT HON. THE EARL JERMYN, M.P.
THE REV. LAMBERT B. LARKING, M.A.
PETER LEVESQUE, ESQ. F.S.A.
SIR FREDERICK MADDEN, K.H., F.R.S.
FREDERIC OUVRY, ESQ. Treas.S.A.
WILLIAM J. THOMS, ESQ. F.S.A., *Secretary.*
WILLIAM TITE, ESQ. M.P., F.R.S.
REV. JOHN WEBB, M.A., F.S.A.

# INTRODUCTION.

THE writer of the following diary was member of a family settled in Suffolk from the time of Edward III., when Peter le Rous is named as owner of the manor of Dennington. The sixth in descent from him, Sir William Rous, was father of Sir Anthony, who purchased Henham Hall, still the family seat, and died in 1547. His son Thomas was alike the ancestor of the diarist and of the Earl of Stradbrooke, the present representative of the elder branch of the family. The following pedigree is compiled from one preserved in the archives of the Earl of Stradbrooke, to whom I am indebted for its communication, collated with another in the Heralds' College, and augmented by additional information from Davy's Suffolk Collections in the British Museum, and from the parish registers of Weeting and Downham in Norfolk, and of Hessett in Suffolk, the residences of that branch of the house to which the diarist belongs:

Peter le Rous, of Dennington, temp. Edw. III.=........

Seventh in descent from him is sir Anthony=Agnes, dau. of sir Thomas Blennerhassett, of Friends Hall, co. Norfolk.
Rous, of Dennington, who bought Henham Hall; died 1547.

Catherine, dau. of=Thomas Rous, of Dennington; died 1573.=Anne, dau. and coheir of sir Nicholas Hare, of Bruisyard, Master of the Rolls.
Giles Hansard.

*a*

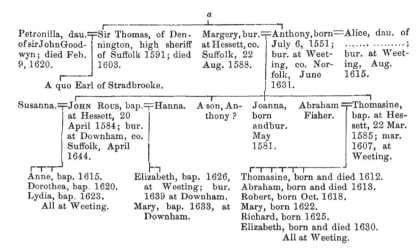

*a*

| Petronilla, dau. of sir John Goodwyn; died Feb. 9, 1620. | ┬ | Sir Thomas, of Dennington, high sheriff of Suffolk 1591; died 1603. | Margery, bur. at Hessett, co. Suffolk, 22 Aug. 1588. | ┬ | Anthony, born July 6, 1551; bur. at Weeting, co. Norfolk, June 1631. | ═ | Alice, dau. of ...... .........; bur. at Weeting, Aug. 1615. |

A quo Earl of Stradbrooke.

| Susanna. ═ | John Rous, bap. at Hessett, 20 April 1584; bur. at Downham, co. Suffolk, April 1644. | ┬ | Hanna. | A son, Anthony? | Joanna, born and bur. May 1581. | Abraham Fisher. | ┬ | Thomasine, bap. at Hessett, 22 Mar. 1585; mar. 1607, at Weeting. |

| Anne, bap. 1615. Dorothea, bap. 1620. Lydia, bap. 1623. All at Weeting. | Elizabeth, bap. 1626, at Weeting; bur. 1639 at Downham. Mary, bap. 1633, at Downham. | Thomasine, born and died 1612. Abraham, born and died 1613. Robert, born Oct. 1618. Mary, born 1622. Richard, born 1625. Elizabeth, born and died 1630. All at Weeting. |

The only tangible allusion made by the diarist to his family connections is a mention of his wife,[a] and the notice of the death of his father, Anthony Rous, in 1631.[b] His own *Christian* name does not appear throughout, but he is identified with the *John* Rous of the pedigree, by the fact that he was evidently a minister, and that in the early part of the diary he speaks of himself as resident at Weeting, whilst in the latter part he speaks of " our town of Downham;" the period of the removal coinciding with that at which we find, from the parish registers, that John Rous left Weeting for Downham or its neighbourhood. Another curious coincidence strengthens this identification,—the handwriting in the parish registers of Weeting, up to the period of the death of Anthony Rous, is precisely that employed by our diarist, as the formal hand in which he copied out verses and other extracts which abound in the volume.[a]

Of the private history of John Rous, further than it is evolved in the diary itself, the records are extremely slight. He was born at Hessett in Suffolk, to which living his father was instituted in 1579, and his birth probably took place in April 1584, as his father records in the register of Hessett, " Johes Rous, fil. mei Anthonii Rous et Margeriæ, bap. 20 Ap. 1584." A sister was added to the family group the following year; and the diarist also speaks of his brother, of whose birth no record appears. In 1588, when little more than four years of age, he lost his mother. The date at which her place was filled by Alice, second wife of Anthony Rous, does not appear, except that it was previous to 1606, in which year he records the death of " Ann Keys, widow, sister to Alice Rous, my wife." It would appear that Anthony Rous remained at Hessett until the year 1600, when he obtained the appointment to the rectory of the united parishes of Weeting St. Mary and Weeting All Saints, on the presentation of Thomas Wright, by grant from Sir Robert Wingfield and others. A John Rous, probably a member of the same family, was rector of the joint parishes a century previously, from 1503 to 1518, the patronage then being in the hands of the earl of Oxford. Little is known of the collegiate life of John Rous. He was admitted pensioner in Emmanuel College, Cambridge, in 1598, and took his degree of master of arts there in 1607.[b] Of the intermediate gradations

[a] For tracings and extracts from this register, and from that of Downham, as well as for much valuable local information, I am indebted to the courtesy of the Rev. F. Vyvyan Luke, the present curate of Weeting.

[b] These particulars are gathered from the obliging communications of Joseph Romilly, Esq. Registrar of Cambridge, and Dr. Archdall, Master of Emmanuel College.

of his academic career no other notice is preserved; but he seems
to have kept up a correspondence with his *alma mater*; for, scanty
as are the notices in the diary of private persons or affairs, two
allusions occur to Emmanuel College, one to the widow of a Mr.
Cudworth, one of the fellows, the other to the death of Dr. Chaderton, the Master of the College.[a]   He also mentions the election
of Buckingham as chancellor of Cambridge in 1626; the appearance there of the plague; the visit of the King and Queen in 1633;
the suicide of Dr. Butts, vice-chancellor, shortly afterwards; and
other particulars of local history connected with the town and university.[b]   Graduation at Cambridge did not involve permanency of
abode there; and it seems probable that John Rous was only an
occasional resident, as from the year 1601, when he was only seven-
teen, we find him residing with his father at Weeting, and exercising
his beautiful calligraphy, as the rector's amanuensis, in the registry
books, from that period down to 1631, the date of the decease
of Anthony Rous.   Before that time, on September 21st, 1623, he
was appointed minister of the small village of Santon Downham, now
consisting only of the church and two houses, adjoining the parish
of Weeting;[c] but he seems to have still lived with his father, probably on account of his great age and consequent infirmities, for the
old man survived almost to the completion of his eightieth year.

During the period of his residence at Weeting, various domestic
changes befel our diarist, none of which, however, are recorded or
even alluded to, by himself.   He married, became the father of three

[a] Pp. 80, 99.

[b] Pp. 3, 51, 52, 56, 70.

[c] The name on the Bishop's registry is *William* Rous; but the register was incorrectly
kept, as appears from the date of 1627 instead of 1631 being assigned as that of the
death of Anthony Rous.   The burial register of Downham distinctly names him John.

daughters, buried a first wife, and replaced her by a second, who brought him a fourth daughter. From his frequent mention of attendances at sessions and assizes, it seems probable that he held a commission, as justice of the peace.

The parsonage-house at Weeting, where he probably lived at this period, is still the residence of the minister of Weeting. " I cannot help fancying," writes the Rev. F. Vyvyan Luke, its present occupant, " that the very room in which I am now penning these lines, was the one in which a portion of the diary was written. It is a part of the old parsonage; and, though modernised externally, yet the party walls, I conjecture, must go back almost to the time of Edward I. for their date. It evidently was the 'keeping-room' of former days. Some years ago I removed the old brick floor, in order to fit it for a study; underneath I came to a thick bed of clay, embedded in which were bones of almost every description of animal used for food; beef, mutton pork, rabbits, fowls, &c. speaking most forcibly of the habits of olden time."—" At that period," he adds, " the country must have presented a far different appearance from what it does now. At present it is becoming well wooded, being inclosed some years ago by act of parliament; but then it was a wild, open, sandy heath, bordering the forest, the resort of the bustard and other game long extinct."

On the decease of Anthony Rous, his son left Weeting. It seems likely that he resided, not at Downham itself, the sphere of his duties, which was a very unimportant place, and where no trace or tradition of a parsonage-house exists, but in Brandon, the neighbouring town, several times mentioned in the diary, where in a particular building, called " the ministers' house," several of the clergy of the adjacent rural parishes took up their abode. About this period he visited

London.[a]   We also find an allusion to his having travelled as far
as Geneva, but to the date of this more formidable journey no clue
is given: he mentions it casually, when quoting, amongst other
verses, a distich of his own upon "Glorious Geneva."[b]   In 1633,
we find him again settled in his own locality; in that year is recorded the baptism at Downham of his fifth daughter, Mary, and
there also in 1639 he buried his fourth daughter, Elizabeth.   In
1640 he is again in London, where he mentions his attendance at
St. Paul's on the Fast-day, Nov. 17.[c]   The interlarding of speeches
in Parliament and other public matters gives rise to the presumption that he remained some time a spectator of the stirring events
then daily transpiring in the metropolis.   After this time, we have
no particulars of his domestic history till we come to the entry in the
register of Downham, which, under the year 1644, records as fol-
lows: "John Rous, clerk and minister of Downham, son of Anthony Rous, late minister of Weeting, Norfolk, buried April 4th."

The register at Downham is not an original but a transcript,
made by Mr. Knowle, curate in 1799; the handwriting of John
Rous cannot therefore be traced to the close of his career, which ter-
minated before he had completed his sixtieth year.

We now turn from the man to his works.   The original diary, as
it lies before me, is a small quarto volume of 176 pages, in two distinctly marked handwritings, though both evidently by the same
hand, a current style used for ordinary details, and a formal one for
extracts, more particularly verses.   The present is evidently the con-
tinuation of some previous diary, to which he once alludes, which
seems to have contained 198 folios, as the present MS. bears a

---

[a] He speaks of this visit, in 1636, as taking place "some years ago."   P. 84.
      [b] P. 73.                                          [c] P. 103.

foliation as well as pagination, reaching from folio 199 to 286. The diarist mentions " my first long note-book, covered with redder forrell." He also speaks of his " notes of 1612," [a] and of " a folio paper book," in which he recorded a judicial sentence passed on four robbers ; also of " my great book," seemingly an account of Parliamentary affairs ;[b] but of none of these has any trace been discovered. The diary does not give the impression of a work prepared for the public, but rather of a private record of facts, &c. which the writer wished to preserve for his own use. He carefully committed to paper such popular skits [c] and satirical verses as came within his notice, several of which, it is believed, are here printed for the first time, and some of them show strongly the current popular feeling of the times. Amongst the most curious of these productions are " The Times' New Churchman;" " The Dialogue between two Zelots;" " The Dismal Summons to the Doctors' Commons;" " God have mercy, good Scot;" " The Scholar's Complaint;" and " The Mass Priest's Lamentation."[d] His own sympathies by no means went with some of these railing rhymes. On one occasion he says that he *hates* them, and only preserves them as a " precedent of the times."

He paid considerable attention to general literature, more especially to that of a religious controversial nature, which would naturally engage the attention of a clergyman, and he occasionally inserts documents of a miscellaneous or political character; such of these as are already known in print, have been omitted, but several of those inserted are new and curious. Such is the letter

[a] P. 45.  [b] Pp. 76, 113.  [c] See pp. 8, 26, 31, 54, 80.
[d] Pp. 78, 106, 109, 110, 115, 118.
[e] Pp. 5, 6, 35, 37, 54, 63, 67, 70, 76, 80.

on the death of the Duke of Buckingham;[a] that from the Duke of Orleans to the Pope;[b] and that from " the Devil to the Pope."[c]

His tone of feeling on the leading struggle between monarchy and democracy was remarkably moderate. At first he looked upon the King's character favourably,[d] but the current of events induced a leaning towards the Parliamentary cause. He was never a warm partizan on either side, and he freely interlards his memoranda of public events with farming notices,[e] on weather and crops, and the gossip of a rural neighbourhood.[f] He seems to have had also a *penchant* for heraldry, as the latter part of the MS. is written on paper which has evidently been intended for memoranda of coats of arms. Several of the pages are headed " Armes, whose by view," and the margin contains lists of armorial charges, &c. with the capitals A. B. E. G. O. S. V. supposed to specify the colours, &c. Argent, Blue, Ermine, Gules, Or, Sable, Vert.

The frequent use of Latin quotations, and the insertion of Latin verses, prove that our author had a scholar-like acquaintance with that language, and he also occasionally quoted French. In fact, we may regard him as a respectable type of a country clergyman of the times, who through his " loophole of retreat" could peep at the tumultuous world beyond, " see the great Babel, and not feel the crowd," and record the impressions, which, after the lapse of more than two centuries, are brought into unexpected publicity.

For the permission to print this MS. I am indebted to the courtesy of Dawson Turner, Esq., the well known-collector of autographs and Norfolk antiquities, to whose library it belongs, and who kindly permitted its transcript for the Camden Society.

[a] P. 27.   [b] P. 77.   [c] P. 38.
[d] See pp. 11, 19, 49.   [e] Pp. 24, 56, &c.   [f] Pp. 22, 45, 56, 60, 66, &c.

# DIARY OF JOHN ROUS.

His comming to the crowne was very joyous to the well-affected, but to Papists not very welcome.

Of the matche with France then on foote, rumours were diverse, yet at length arrived in England Mary sister to Lewes XIII. of France, about Whitsontide. Newes of her arrivall, and the occurrences thereof, was very litle and very uncertaine in Norfolke, by the reason of the plague beginning to be hote in London, so that the parliament assembled was kept at Oxford, and travaile was dangerous.

This summer the King was Westward in progresse, where he visited and viewed his navie at Plimmouth, the greatest that ever England sent out, the expectation thereof being extraordinary; but in the ende all came to nothing but this, an arrivall at Cales[a] in Spaine, with the taking of a forte or two, and then a shamefull returne. Where the faulte was, time may fully discover.[b]

The plague caused Michaelmas terme to be kept at Reding in Barkeshire.

---

[a] Cades, Cadiz.

[b] The Admiral, Edward Cecill, lord Wimbledon, having a large fleet under his command, and meeting with little opposition, was much blamed for not doing more execution. Rushworth, pt. i. p. 196.

In the ende of this summer were many rumors of letters taken that discovered trechery of Papists, readie to have received (after some way made) marquis Spinola at Harwich and Ipswich, who had great forces (as was said) together at Dunkirke. Soldiers out of Suffolk and Essex lay in garrison at Langher point, and this feare hath caused strong fortes to be builte there.[a]

Proclamations came forth against Papists; and some stricter courses with them, for theire arrerages to the King, and for executing of penall statutes, were set on foote and doe continue.[b]

1626. Our trayned soldiers were often exercised by Captaines chosen. The long continued peace with Spaine (being nowe 1625 in the breaking of) caused such security in our townes and ordinary shippes, that many had sould away theire ordinance, being nowe enforced to buy newe, the advantage whereof the Dunkirkers haue made use of, and troubled our seas, taken our shippes, and feared our merchants and smaller sea townes, to the causing of much discontented rumour in the country.

Sir Edward Cooke (late lord Cooke) was chosen knight of the shire for Norfolk, (as before in the former parliament ended at Oxford,) but for prevention he and some others free speakers in parliament (*ut dicitur*) were made high sheriffes;[c] so that in the beginning of this parliament (begunne in the ende of 1625) much adoe there was about this pointe; making way, as was thought, for the utter bringing under of parliament power, and the jealousie betwixt the King's prerogative and the freedome of the country, with the Parliamentary power, encreasing (by the sending of the earle of Arundle to the Tower, the King refusing to shewe his reason), there

[a] Landguard or Langer Fort, near Harwich. See Rushworth, pt. i. p. 195.

[b] See the Petition of the Commons against recusants, with the king's Answers, in Rushworth, vol. i. pp. 181—6. Also Fœdera, Hague edit. vol. viii. pt. i. pp. 128, 189.

[c] The others were sir Robert Philips and sir Thomas Wentworth. The office of high sheriff incapacitated the person from becoming member of Parliament so long as he held it, and was therefore a penalty to those who were ambitious of parliamentary distinction.

was much griefe in the country. At the last it came to this. Sir Edward Cooke was a parliament man, but by the parliament house (to satisfye the King) forbidden to meddle untill he were called. The earle of Arundell, whose faulte was (*ut ferunt*) a presuming to steale a matche of his sonne the lord Matrevers with the duke of Lennox daughter,[a] wherein the King was interested, entending to marry her within fewe dayes to the earle of Argile's sonne, (as his father king James had directed,) was set at libertie.[b]

This Parliament hath as yet, June 1626, bent almost wholly against the duke of Buckingham, (who lately, after the death of the earle of Suffolk, was chosen Chancelor of Cambridge, some agents, *ut dicunt*, pressing others for theire voices with him,) being questioned at Parliament, to the greate wonder of the country, considering the strange, usuall, and bould reportes that be made of him; which, if true, 'tis pity he liveth; if otherwise, God graunte him a true cleering.[c]

About June 11, the Parliament ·was dissolved, nothing being done. The lord keeper, sir Thomas Coventry, being (*ut dicitur*) earnest with the King, upon his knees, to have it continued.

The cause, as farre as country intelligence could telle us, was that the nether house delayed the grante of subsidies untill the duke had beene tried, which the King was against. The reporte that the King sending to them to conclude for subsidies, with promise that they should afterward sitte againe, they put it to voices, and there were one hundred more against the grante then for it, is not contradicted. Presently after the Parliament's dissolution, the newes was, that the duke had sent to the Parliament sitting; others say, spake himselfe to the Parliament, in way of answere for himselfe (which

---

[a] Elizabeth, eldest daughter of Esme Stuart, duke of Lennox. For particulars of this love-match, see Court and Times of Charles I. vol. i. pp. 86, 90.

[b] See Rushworth, pt. i. pp. 363 et seq.

[c] See Rushworth, pt. i. pp. 371-4. Here follow the Articles presented by the earl of Bristol against lord Conway and the duke of Buckingham, which it is not thought desirable to reprint, they being already printed in Rushworth, pt. i. pp. 264-6, and elsewhere.

answere is in writing), not denying many articles, but intreating favourable construction, as, namely, his offensive incontinency, that it might be imputed to his youth; and the miscarriage of maine busines to error of judgment, which the happiest counsellor of all is subjecte to, &c. There was it seemeth an offer made to permitte the duke to a triall by his peeres at the King's Bench barre, but it was refused, both because it was at this time (thus to be granted) an impeachment to the honour and equality of a parliamentary triall, and for that it is thought, *rege favente*, the peeres might have beene his speciall frends if not creatures; unto which it is added by reporte, that if he had beene found guilty, yet all had beene nothing, for he had, (they say,) three pardons, one from king James, one from king Charles, at his first beginning to reigne, and one other, sealed,

Jun. very lately. I sawe a proclamation at this time running thus : By the King. His majestie being given intelligence that certaine of the House of Commons (committees) did entende to present to him a copie of remonstrance, &c. which copie his majestie refused to be presented to him; the House having refused a most equall tryall of matters objected, at the honourable courte of the King's Bench, and his majestie understanding that they meante to disperse copies of the same remonstrance; and for that it containeth in it things touching the honour of the late deceased King, the nowe King reigning, and the credite of a great Peere of this realme, therefore his majestie forbiddes all his subjects the keeping of the same remonstrance, charging them immediatly upon sight of it to burne it, otherwise, if it be found with any, that they expecte his displeasure according to the qualitie of this facte, &c.[a] This proclamation having the third person altogether, " his majestie," never having " we," or " our pleasure," or the like, had yet no counsellors' handes to it, being subscribed, " God save the King," the printer added.

About this time there came forth diverse proclamations; as,

---

[a] Printed in Fœdera, vol. viii. pt. ii. p. 65 ; date 17th June, 1626.

I. That men should forbeare writing of controversies; it restraining and aiming at controversies lately on foote against Montagu,[a] who wrote "Apello ad Cesarem," and before that, "The Gagge."[b] This booke hath beene answered by Doctor Carleton, bishop of Chichester;[c] by Mr. Rous, Esqu., of Essex;[d] by Mr. Yates, late preacher in Norwich;[e] by one Mr. H. Burton,[f] and by others. I did see 4 or 5 sheetes of a booke in the presse, whereof the copie was taken from the printer by the bishop of London. This was (some say) Dr. Sutcliffe's;[g] but I am sure it was tarte and bitter as gall, surpassing Martin Marprelate, &c.; it called Montagu "Mounte-banke" and "Runnagate Dicke," &c. I commende not this straine, but leave all to the censure of the wise, who may see more then I can what danger this "Apello ad Cesarem" hath done and may doe. One other proclamation was to prohibite saylers to goe out, and to commande a readines for the King's service.[h] A rumour there was nowe of a Spanish fleete, some fearing, and some contemptuously and lightly regarding the force of it and the reporte.

The proclamation restraining controversies and newe opinions

[a] Rushworth, pt. i. p. 412; Fœdera, vol. viii. pt. ii. p. 64, date 16th June, 1626.

[b] Richard Montagu, afterwards Bishop of Norwich and Chichester. His books are entitled, "A Gagg for the new Gospell? No; a New Gagg for an Old Goose, or an Answer to a late Abridgment of Controversies and Belyar of the Protestants' Doctrine." 4to. London, 1624; and, "Appello Cæsarem, A Just Appeale from Two Unjust Informers." Lond. 1625.

[c] In a quarto pamphlet of 236 pages, entitled "An Examination of those things wherein the Author of the late Appeale holdeth the Doctrines of the Pelagians and Arminians to be the Doctrines of the Church of England." 4to. Lond. 1626.

[d] Francis Rous: "Doctrine of King James, of the Church of England, and of the Catholic Church, shewed to be the same in Points of Predestination, Freewill, and Certainty of Salvation." 4to. Lond. 1626.

[e] "Ibis ad Cæsarem; or, an Answer to Mr. Montagu's Appeal in the Points of Arminianism and Popery against the Doctrine of the Church of England." 4to. Lond. 1626.

[f] "A Plea to an Appeal traversed dialoguewise." 4to. Lond. 1626.

[g] Matthew Sutcliffe: "Unmasking of a Masse-monger, or a Vindication of St. Augustine's Confessions from the Calumnies of a late Apostate." 4to. Lond. 1626.

[h] Fœdera, vol. viii. pt. ii. p. 65, date 18th June, 1626.

contrary to the peace of the church, &c., was used by some bishop
to the suppressing of those that had confuted Montague (or rather
abused), whereas Montague hath but only fathered his opinion upon
the Church of England in his blinde conceite.   Witnesse " Novem
assertiones orthodoxæ," Mr. Rogers' Tables and Exposition of the
Articles,[a] the continuall determinings at the scholes Cambridge
and Oxford, and the confutations of Montague by Bishop Carleton
by Mr. Rous, Mr. Yates, &c.

A third proclamation was about such as had the king's evill to
repaire to the courte at a certaine time of the yeere.[b]

There was a proclamation of a fast about August 2,[c] some cause
alledged as, namely, the contagion spreading in the country, &c.
but the chiefe troubles abroad and invasion at home threatned by
potent enemie, etc., of which what wise men thought I leave to
Some thought it a policy to drawe monies. others to utter.   I am sure at Bury assizes and Norfolk, also at Thet
ford (the plague being at Norwich), letters came and justices met
but nothing was obteined.   It was said that at the first there was
endeavor to have gotten by authority the subsidies agreed upon at
the parliament, but not granted because it was untimely broken up
but after it came to a persuasion by the justices for a voluntary yeeld
ing of so much, or neere so much, &c.   Privy seales had this
summer beene talkte of.

Thomas Scotte, " Vox Populi," was slaine about June or July.

[a] Thomas Rogers : "The Faith, Doctrine, and Religion professed and protected in
the realme of England, expressed in xxxix Articles, the said Articles analysed, with
Propositions, and the Propositions proved to be agreeable both to the written Word of
God, and to the Confessions of all the neighbour Churches Christianly reformed." 4to
Lond. 1629.

[b] Fœdera, vol. viii. pt. i. p. 86; date 18 June, 1625.  It might probably be re-issued
this year in the same form.

[c] It was for the 5th of July in town, and August 2nd in the country. See Fœdera
vol. viii. pt. ii. p. 68; date June 30, 1626.

[d] " Vox Populi, or Newes from Spayne," 1620, the Second part, 1624, by Thomas
Scott, B.D. English minister at Utrecht.  The account of his death was published in " A
Briefe Relation of the Murder of Mr. Thomas Scott, Preacher of God's Word an

About September 29, I sawe a proclamation which seemed to impute the not payment of privy seales to some miscarriage, &c. and not to the subjects' disloyaltie; withall, also notice was given that there were other projects, wherefore the King had taken order that such monies as were paid upon privy seales or benevolence, should be presently repayed.[a]

In Suffolk a benevolence was yeelded and in parte paid.

The King's navy went forth about Michaelmas.

This summer was greate preparation and building about the forte at Langer Pointe; and upon some displeasure the earle of Warwicke, Lieftenant of Essex and the chiefe overseer, was turned out of his offices, and the worke forsaken.   September —, sir John Rous, of Henham,[b] had spoken something of the duke at the last parliament, and he was turned out of his offices.

The French were all shipped away from the queene.

The king of Denmarke had a greate overthrowe.[c]

Sir Jacob Asteley was said to be made generall of all the English in the Netherlands.

Newes came in October of count Mansfeld, that he had given diverse overthrowes to the emperor's parte, and slaine the duke of Friedland in the field.[d]   Newes is newes.   Many corantoes confirmed an overthrowe given to the duke of Friedland.

During Michaelmas terme, a projecte was on foote for 5 subsidies, to be paid all at once.   The judges would neither yeeld to this for to be lawe or conscience; and sir Randolph Crewe, chief justice of the king's bench, was suspended from his office.   This was prose-

Bachelor of Divinity, committed by John Lambert, soldier of the garrison of Utrecht, the 18th of June, 1626." 4to. Lond. 1628. See also Court and Times of Charles I. vol. i. p. 123.

[a] Fœdera, vol. viii. pt. ii. p. 94 ; date 22nd Sept. 1626.

[b] This is the nephew of the diarist, son of his elder brother Thomas.

[c] He was defeated by Tilly, Aug. 27th.

[d] A false report ; the story of Wallenstein's murder in 1634 is too well known to need an allusion.

8

DIARY OF JOHN ROUS. [A.D. 1626.

cuted by all helpes, as persuasions from the clergie; and about th
middle of December at Bury by the earles of Shrewsbury and Suf
folke, &c., and it was generally yielded, and so in Norfolk.

The French stayed our marchants' shippes.

The queenes lutener, a Frenchman, layd in the Tower, for tha
he had a pistoll charged with double bullett, to kill the duke, *u*
*dicitur*.[a] Newes in February, that the king of France (who had stayed
our shippes that went for wines, with theire ordonance, whereupon
letters of marke were granted against the French,[b]) had proclaimed
open warres against England; or rather, as some say, had begunne
to levie a great armie for his own defence, perhaps against England
Sir John Heviningham, being in the Marshalsey for refusing to pay
the 5 subsidies, the newes held currant that 4 or 5 shires held out
whole; as Lancashire, Cheshire, Derby, &c.

Of 5 Lord Chiefe Justices of the king's bench, living at one time,
Feb. 1626, stilo n̄to,[c]

Lerned Cooke and Montagu,
S<sup>r</sup> James Leigh, and honest Crewe,
Two preferd, two put beside,
There's *now in place* sir Nicholas Hide.[d]

Now skipt in.

---

[a] His name was Galtier, but this was not his real offence. See Court and Times of
Charles I. vol. i. pp. 183, 186, 189, 190.

[b] See Fœdera, vol. viii. pt. ii. pp. 119, 182.    [c] Stilo nostro : the old style.

[d] There are other readings of this popular skit :—

Learned Cooke and Montagu,
Grave Leigh, and honest Crew,
Two preferred, two set aside,
Then starts up sir Nicholas Hyde.

Another has—

Learned Coke, curt Montagu,
The aged Leigh, and honest Crew.

See Court, &c. of Charles I. vol. i. p. 199; and Yonge's Diary, p. 100.

Sir Edward Coke and sir Randolph Crewe were both displaced during the reign of
James I. Sir Henry Montagu, afterwards earl of Manchester, had been made lord
president of the council by that king, and sir James Ley, afterwards earl of Marlborough, lord high treasurer.

March 15.  Newes that the king of France having gotten some company into Rochell deceitfully, there arose a sudden conflicte, many of the Protestants slaine, yet the towne not surprised, but the king's forces approching to the towne warde.  Of 130 ships stayed in France, it is thought we shall have none sent home, but all are employed in the siege of Rochell; in liewe of which ships, we have taken some 30 base ships of the French.   Some say our navy shall aide Rochell.

That the earle of Lincolne is in the Tower, about the subsidies; and the earle of Essex sent for by pursevants.  That Yorkeshire, Lincolnshire, Lancashire, Derbyshire, Northamptonshire, Leicester-shire, with others, and Wales, doe wholie denie this subsidie.  That the Hollanders have sent messengers to demande restitution of some-thing the duke withholdeth; and, in case of deniall, doe say that they are to stande on theire owne feete, and to grant letters of marke to take so much from us.

That there is proclamation that no merchant shall trade, in any kind, with Spaine, upon paine of [a]

That the Dunkerkers have taken 50 coliers of ours.

That the earle of Warwicke's pinnace hath taken ij ships of 10,000*l*. prise, comming now into the Thames to the Tower ward: whereof 1000 is the king's, 1000 the duke's; or the tenth for the king, the ninth for the admirall; the rest is the adventurers'.

That letters of marke are daily given out against the Dunkirkers, as the sole helpe our haven towens have to helpe themselves.

May.  Newes about Witsontide was that the earles of Warwick 1627, in May. and Essex were gone to sea, with a small navy of perhaps xx ships, having letters of marke.  Also, that we have had from the French full satisfaction for our ships stayed; and proclamation was made

---

[a] Of his ships being seized as prizes.  Fœdera, vol. viii. pt. ii. p. 156 ; date 4th March, 1626-7.  The proclamation prohibits the furnishing the Spaniards with provisions or munition of war.

that all that had sustained losse by the French should,  upon proofe
of theire losses made to the Councell, be satisfyed out of the prise
taken from the French.[a]

Proclamation prohibiting all trade with the French.[b]

Also that the duke was to goe forth, with a greate navy of the
King's ships, of his owne, and others, above 100.

That the prisoners for refusing the subsidies imposed are yet in
prison, and others brought in unto them, out of Norfolk,  Lincolnshire, and other places.

That captaine Penniton, being abroad with letters of marke, had
by a wile taken and sent home 20 French ships at one time.   He
went in among theire ships with French flagges, and then, being
once in the middest of them, he shewed himselfe enemie, and
so caused the most of them to yeeld.[c]

June 15.  The newes was, about the last of June, that the duke was gone
out from Portsmouth, with 90 saile of ships.   This newes was confirmed from Cambridge commencement.

July 7.  About July 7, it was rumoured that he had taken St. Martin's, in
a little island lying before Rochelle in France.

Sept. 20.  The rumour was true, but the whole island of Ree (de Rey) was
not taken; for the citadell commanding the towne was thought not
to be taken.   September 20.

Sept.  A towne called the Grolle, in Gelderland, was taken lately by the
prince of Aurange.

Sept.  Greate diversity of reportes about an overthrowe given to Tilly
of 8000 men by the king of Denmarke; some affirming it a tale,
some saying it was true.

Sept. 24.  There were, on the Bell corner post at Thetford, a proclamation
to give the forfeitures of papists, &c. to the erle of Sunderland,

[a] See Fœdera, vol. viii. pt. ii. p. 134.

[b] Fœdera, vol. viii. pt. ii. p. 175, 12th May, 1627.

[c] See Court and Times of Charles I. vol. i. pp. 221, 228 ; and Yonge's Diary, p. 105.
These prizes were sold by the King to Burlamachi for 150,000*l.*

lord president at Yorke, to be taken in diverse northerne shires, towards the mainteyning of vi. good ships of warre, to cleere the northerne costes of pirates.[a]  Another for transporting of corne to the isle of Ree, or Rochell, given to all free borne or free denizens and Rochellers, so that obligation cautionary were put in for delivery of the same corne, and the sale of it at those places, to be knowne by certificate from the duke Lord Generall, the duke of Subise, and others commissioners abiding at Ree.[b]

A proclamation over the same post at Thetford, signifying that the King had revived a commission that was determined by his father's death, about the enquiry for all newe offices and newe fees in all the courts ecclesiasticall or civill; information to be given hereof, at Westminster, to the commissioners there.[c] Nov. 3.

At Brandon, mr. Paine of Riddlesworth,[d] mr. Howlet sitting by, in Grimes hall, tould me that a Frenchman, sir Thomas Woodhouse' man, tould him that one Cornelis, or the like, an enginer that went with the duke and yet was now at London, did tell him that the forte was not to be wonne but by starving; and that it was many times victualled, &c.  This said mr. Paine was *oculatus testis*, &c., and when I went about to tell him of the mappe I sawe of the forte, and what was delivered in it, especially about the ships riding against the forte, and of the provision made by masters [e] for the staying of boates that should victuall it, he would not heare it by any meanes; but fell in generall to speake distastfully of the voyage, and then of our warre with France, which he would make our King the cause of, for not establishing the queene in her joynture; to which I answered that I was able, with a little looking, to shewe statute lawe requiring such performances of a queene before

Nov. 6. or Dutchman

he heard of one *oculatum testem* indeede as 'tis said.

---

[a] Fœdera, vol. viii. pt. ii. p. 191, date 27th June, 1627.

[b] Fœdera, vol. viii. pt. ii. p. 207, date 18th August, 1627.

[c] Ibid. p. 213, date 12th October, 1627.

[d] In Gillcross hundred, co. Norfolk.

[e] "Mastes" in MS.

her crowning, as I thought she had refused.  I further said that, a
she is, there might be danger, lest, being queene, king Charle
should be stabbed, as Henry IV. late in France; and then th
queene regent might marre all.  And the conclusion was, that
thought it fowle for any man, not having seene the articles, to la
the blame upon our owne King and state.  I tould them I woul
alwaies speake the best of that our King and state did, and think
the best too, till I had good groundes.  They fell upon ould dis
contents, for the parliament being crossed, expenses, hazard o
ships, &c.  I answered that our expenses were small to Spaine's
and in greate designes there must be hazard, &c.  I sawe hereb
that which I had seen often before, viz.: Men be disposed to speak
the worst of state businesses, and to nourish discontente, as if ther
were a false carriage in all these things, which if it were so, wha
would a false hearte rather see then an insurrection?  a way where
unto these men prepare.

Why did we
leave the Pala-
tinate and fall
fowle with
France ?

About the last of October, came divers Scots, about 30, from th
coaste neare Yarmouth, saying that there came 30 ships of them
well appointed with victuals and munition, besides 5000 land sol
diers, to goe to the duke; and being dispersed by a storme, and som
of them driven on Norfolk coaste, they landed, intending to ride t
the King, to let him knowe, &c.  The presse was yet on foote fo
men to goe with my lord of Holland.  At this there was som
speech of the forte being taken; but the current is so strong agains
the duke's honour, and the uncertainty of reportes such, that few
did matter it.  The reporte was that the duke had lost most of ou
men, and that our ships were much hurte, and the duke was re
turned.

The evill newes was so current, that one told me that the Frencl
from the forte shot our men, and kilde them as they looked out.  I
replied thus: " Belike our men are fooles to put out theire heades
and the French very watchfull to be so readie."

Either October 28, or November 4, being Sunday, there was a

October.

Octob.

Nov. 3.

Nov. 17.

Tempest.

greevous tempest of wind in the night, which caused much ship-
wracke upon the coasts of Norfolk and Suffolk, with other places.

Upon the 24th of November was a like tempestuous windie night.

About the 16th of November the duke was come to London, and Duke.
had relinquished the isle of Rees, and lost, at his comming away,
many brave captaines and other, commanders and captains, some
42 or more, &c.

This newes made much muttering, and caused much suspition,
as may be seene by this tale caried about,—that the governor of the
isle, before the duke's comming, made a great feast to the best of
the nobles and others with him, and asked if they would stand for
theire king, if the king of England came; they answered yes. To
this tale I answered, that, granting it true, yet I could not well thinke
our comming to be revealed upon trechery; for many nobles,
about 22, were slaine of the French, &c. It was answered that they
were protestants, almost all; yet I proceeded, and said that the
governor might say as much, from a meere supposall that our long
preparing navy was for Rees, partly because France and we were
before fallen at oddes, and Monsieur Soubees, from whom the king
of France had taken this island, was at that time in the English
courte, or in the English navy.

The busines nowe on foot betwixt England and France is of greate Nov. 26.
consequence, and the slaughter in Rees will breed but evill bloud,
&c. The Jesuites, I believe, have made it high time for England
to helpe the protestants ; whom to suppresse, the Spanish faction
helpeth what they can, and so that is, &c., the king of England
might have no frends, and Spain the aide of catholikes in case, &c.:
*qui potest capere, capiat:* herein may be double policy; one as
before, the other to diverte us from helping the protestants of Germany &c. Well! be it so! yet there is no councell against God.

The newes was that a mortality, both at sea and land, fell amongst Feb. or Mar. 1.
the enemies that besieged Rochell, so that the siege was removed. Rochell was yet
It was a policy to prevent discredit perhaps.  Corne cheape.  Barly besieged in
July.

betweene iiij*s.* and v*s.* the combe.    Rie vj*s.* viij*d.*, yea lesse.    Wheat x*s.* or little more.

This winter, many soldiers, the remainder at Rees, were billetted in these partes, Essex, Suffolk, and Norfolk; in greater townes Irish men most of them.

Jan. Wind.

Wondrous sore winde January 27, and 28 greater, overturning many buildings, barnes, and other; to the losse of many thousand pounds.

March 17.    The parliament beganne.    Sir John Heviningham being chosen knight for Norfolk, soone after his delivery from the Marshalsey.

See one, page 42. [p. 29.]

Newes was that the duke [a] was in the Tower, and strange rimes and songs came abroade before the time.

Jesuites taken in a vault at Clerkenwell in London.[b]

A public fast for the good successe of the Parl., at London before Easter, in the country on the Munday after Easter Moonday.

Newes at London, May 3, was that the parliament[c] did stand to have (beyonde the King's worde) an acte for the confirmation of all theire immunities and freedomes, which were granted to the subjects in Magna Charta &c., with an explanation of those grants.    That the Scottish lords were come to London, after some fear of a commotion, upon the King's enquiry for abbey lands there, as concealed from the crowne &c.

That the Dutch ships from the East Indies were staid at Portsmouth, brought in by our King's ships, and paid a greate summe for wrong offered to our English, yet lesse, it is thought, because many thousand pounds worth of goods were embezeled away while the shippes remayned in our men's custody at Portsmouth.    That the returne from St. Christopher's Iland was five for one, or much more.    That the earle of Warwicke is to have a ship newe builte, whose timber, with the bare workemanship (iron excepted), must

---

[a] Duke of Buckingham.

[b] See "The Discovery of the Jesuits' College at Clerkenwell," published in the second volume of the Camden Miscellany.

[c] The diarist here inserts the King's speech and other speeches in parliament, which are printed in Rushworth.

cost xxij hundred poundes; it must be fleeter, drawing lesse water
then ordinary, and is to be made at Woodbridge.ᵃ  Since the former
newes, there followed the newes of the earle of Denbigh, formerly
vicount Fielding, who, it is said, married the duke's sister, that came
from Rochell, where he had been with 20 of the King's ships to relieve it, and wanted there commission to fight with the French
king's navy, &c.  Whereupon one       ᵇ Clerke, sent with letters
to the duke from Denbigh, returned, was put of by the duke, who
said the earle had dishonoured the King and himselfe, &c.  The
newes now was that a French captain reported to the parliament
that they might have relieved Rochell, and would not.

The newes was that on Saturday June 7, the King, who imme- June 11, 13,
diatly before had·made a sadde parliament house, did then graunt ¹⁴·
theire petition about theire liberties, &c.: which was the maine
pointe on foote betweene the King and his subjects.  June 14, I
sawe a writing to this effect: That the King, having beene at the
parliament, immediatly upon his returne to Whitehall, caused his
speech to be penned verbatim, and sent it to be enrolled.  The
summe was thus: he had before given answere to theire long expected petition, such as was for substance as much as now was
desired; which he could not have thought that they would mislike,
being done by so many wise men.  Yet, that they might know that
there was no doublenes in his meaning, he would now give them
satisfaction, in words as before in substance,

> Droit soit faict comme ils desirent.
> Let the right be done as they desire.

That he knew that they would not nor could not wrong his prerogative; that he knewe that the liberties of his subjects was the

---

ᵃ On the river Deben, co. Suffolk.
ᵇ Blank in MS.

strengthning of his prerogative. Having condescended, if it were not now a happie parliament, the sinne was theirs; he was free:[a] when I was writing hereof, Mr. Pratte brought this.

The Kings majesties message to the House of Commons, June 6, 1628.[b]

The King's answere inrolled under the Petition of Right,—"Droit soit faict come il desire par le petition."

After this his Majesty spake a fewe wordes, for which the former leafe shall satisfye.

The heads of the remonstrances which the House of Commons entred to present to His Majesty:—

1. Feare of innovation and change of religion.
2. Innovation of government.
3. Differences in our late employments. [c]
4. Decay of forts.
5. Wante of munition.
6. Decay of trade.
7. Destruction and losse of ships and marriners.
8. No guarding of the seas.
9. That the excessive power of the duke of Buckingham, and the abuses of that power, are the chiefest causes of the evills and danger of the King and kingdome.

These were agreed upon, June 11 or 12, 1628.

Upon the 9th heade were 9 houres spent, whether it should be put into the remonstrance or not; and at last it was carryed against the duke, by 100 voices and more.

June 7. At night, great rejoicing and bonfires in London.

June 14. Sir Roger Townesend, knight of the shire for Norfolk,

---

[a] Rushworth, pt. i. p. 613.

[b] Ibid. p. 610.

[c] The Sloane MS. 826, p. 118, gives a brief digest similar to the present, but the 3rd article is " The feare of foreign designs."

come home 13, said that the parliament ment to goe on where the former parliament lefte, viz. in remonstrance against the duke.   See page 3, 7, 9 ª.   This may well agree with the heades, page 37.ᵇ   The successe is in God.

We received newes that doctor Lambe (called the duke's wisard) was knocked on the heade on the 12th of June or thereabout, at 6 June 18. at night: he and his minion came from a play, and being houted and wondered at by prentises and watermen, was at length battered with stones and otherwise, and so slaine ᶜ.   The devill is dead.

The same time came newes that 5 shippes of Bristoll had relieved Rochell, which the earl of Denbigh, with twenty of the King's ships, did not.   Also that the earle of Dorset was questioned in parliament; he is the duke's great favourite.

That the duke, being at bowles with the King and other noble-men, his hatte was on, which a Scottish man seeing, tooke it of, and threwe it on the ground.   He then offered to spurne him; but said the King, " George, let him alone; he is drunke."   " No," said the Scottish man, " neither drunke nor mad; but a subjecte, as I thought he had beene, of whom if you knewe but what I knowe, you would not so esteeme him as you doe."   The Scottish nobleman (*ut dicunt*) is impris[oned.]

It is reported that one doctor Mannering, of London, was con-vented before the parliament, June 9, for writing and preaching too farre,ᵈ All was the King's &c.; and he was imprisoned; first, as some say, being degraded.

It was also late newes that immediately before the King's good

ª The reference is to the articles against lord Conway and the duke; see p. 3, note c.

ᵇ Heads of the Remonstrance, p. 16.

ᶜ See Rushworth, pt. 1, p. 618.

ᵈ Two obnoxious sermons were preached on the 4th and 29th July,1627,and afterwards published.   They were suppressed by proclamation 24th June, 1628.   The proceedings of parliament against Mainwaring are published in a separate form. 8vo. London, 1709. He was degraded by parliament, but soon afterwards pardoned and promoted by the King.

agreement with the house, many that before had beene strong for the subjects against the excess of prerogative, were turned by the duke, to theire nowe greate griefe and ensuing shame.   Some say that letters from the king of Denmarke and from the lady Elizabeth were a greate cause of the King's consent.   Quere.

These late times have beene troubled with many foolish reportes, such as these:—That the duke caused fower men to watche at a poste, right over against a great ordinary, where they set up a paper to this effecte—50,000*l.* was desired to be lent by the Londoners, which, because they refused, the duke would bring in x thousand soldiers to be billeted (there was a rumor of 12,000 horse to be brought into England), the which paper being pulled downe, these men would have imprisoned the boy that did it; then the Mayor [a] he convented all before him, who, enquiring hereof, said he would raise 12,000 to oppose, and so sent to the duke to knowe whether this were his doing, &c; the duke would not be spoken with, &c.

That the duke was gone to the Tower, and the King accompanying him, for feare he should be throwen over the bridge, or knockte on the heade.   *Ridicula.*   That ships were sent to relieve Rochell, and the Dunkirkers had taken them, and said the duke sent them word where they should meete them, &c.   Former times of late have had more foolish newes then these, related and credited by some that thinke themselves wise.

His Majesties speech to both houses, at the end of this session of parliament, June 26, 1628.[b]

It is commonly said that if the Parliament had not beene thus broken up, ere they did entende to rise, they had declared something openly against the duke.

It is also reported that the question that was about tonnage and poundage, (viz. the Customes), was not to take them away, but to graunte them still to the crowne as formerly they had beene graunted.

[a] Sir Hugh Hammersley.
[b] Printed in Rushworth, vol. i. p. 631.

A secret whispering of some looking towardes the lady Elizabeth is fearfull to be thought of, in regarde of both our soveraigne, and also a wrong to her. Our King's proceedings have caused men's mindes to be incensed, to rove, and projecte, but as for this, it is likely to be meerely the conceite of the multitude, who, if any in these dayes should but among them say, " I pray God keepe men from thoughts upon that lady," would be ready to reporte it, that the whole state were revolting. Blessed Lord God, heale this breache, discover the cause and ground of all our grievances, and settle thou (as thou seest fitte) the heartes of our soveraigne and his subjectes in love and loyaltye together. *Fiat, Domine Jesu!*

I have all this while (discontents have continued long) laboured to make the best construction of all (yea, I had the best construction), that the subjecte might be satisfyed, least discontents should burst out, to our adversaries' rejoicing; yea, I have yeelded reasons for carriage of state busines, so as all should not be knowen, and for the necessityes of greate supplies to the King for the greate affayres on foote. I knowe the error of the vulgar, which is to judge of all things by the event, and therefore to speake according to our harde successe, &c.; but when I heare any alledging that the whole parliament feareth some miscarrying by trechery, &c., then is my mouth stopped, which otherwise hath beene free to speake my reach on the King's behalfe. *Multi mihi testes, præter conscientiam.*

About June 26, the Cession ended, and some statutes printed. All the former passages about immunities printed also. 5 subsidies granted. Parliament prorogued till October.

> And arte returnde againe, with all thy faultes, [a]
> Thou greate Commander of the All goe naughts ? (Argonauts.)

[a] This poem is printed, though with many variations, in the curious collection of Poems on the Duke of Buckingham, edited by Mr. Fairholt for the Percy Society, pp. 19-24. It is from the Sloane MS. 826, f. 31 b. A few lines are omitted in the present version which are found in the other : the readings from the Sloane MS. are given where they seem more correct ; but several instances occur in which the present version will be found to rectify that in the Sloane MS.

And left the Isle behinde the ; what's the matter ?
Did winter make thy chappes beginne to chatter ?
Could not the surging and distempered seas,
Thy queasie [a] stomacke, George, with sweetnes [b] please ?
Or didste thou hasten headlong to prevent
A fruitlesse hope of needfull parliament ?
All these, no question, with a restles motion
Vexte thy besotted soule, as that blacke potion
Turned [c] the noble Scotte, whose names [d] will tell
Thy swolne ambition made his carcase swell.
But there's a reason worse then this, they say ;
The Frenche men beate thee, and thou rannste away.
Can this be true ?  could not thy glorious boastes,
Before thy going, fright them from theire coastes ?
Could not thy Titles scare them ? nor thy Lambe's [e]
Protection safegard the from the French rammes ?
Could not thy mother's masses, nor her crosses,
Nor sorceries, prevent those fatall losses?
Hence [f] we collecte, to those that will be vitious
(Pray who will pray) heaven's not propitious.
Thy sinnes, God's judgments, and the kingdomes curse
Make me admire thy fortunes were no worse.
Happie successe then greate attemptes attendes
When those commande whom vertuous skill commends. [g]
Now I have said enough, I knowe, greate George,
If it were knowne, to make thy power disgorge
Its venome on me ; yet, for all this hate,
Let's at this distance but expostulate.
How could that voyage have such sadde effecte
Without close treachery, or a grosse neglecte ?
Thou had'st a Navy royall did [h] not feare
All the French power, and the coaste could cleere

---

[a] So in MS.  [b] "Sweetmeats," Sloane MS.
[c] "Torture," Sloane MS.
[d] "Titles" in margin, but the Sloane MS. reads more correctly *manes* ; the allusion is to the current suspicion that Buckingham was an agent in the death of James I., and in that of the marquess of Hamilton.  See Mr. Fairholt's note in p. 20 of the "Poems and Songs."
[e] Alluding to doctor Lambe, a favourite of the duke.
[f] "Here," Sloane MS., but *hence* seems the true reading.
[g] This couplet is omitted in Sloane MS.
[h] "need not fear," Sloane MS.

From all invasion, and keepe backe supplie,
The Isle did wholly at thy service lie.
Had every parte of that small tracte of lande
Beene with a slender garde and fielde piece mannde,
Theire enterance sure had been impech'te awhile
As theire approche did eccho o're [a] the Isle.
What, were our captaines streightened in commission
That they thus landed [b] without a prohibition ?
They durst not.   But we heare that they devise [c]
To excuse thy base, ignoble cowardise,
That bruntes of danger could so litle bide
The very brunte [d] did almost make the hide.
And when the bloudy day of Mars was knowne,
And eche one's valour should be chiefly showen,
Was't not a noble parte, and bravelie plaide,
To send a shadowe, in thy armes araide,
To personate the in the battaile ? while
Thou satest environde in a cable coile [e]
Discharging suger pellets.   Had it not beene
More nobly done, by death renowme to winne,
Then in a hempen cable plung'de to be,
With viewe of thy deserved destinie ?
Oh when I thinke of that same fatall fielde,
Wherein so much brave English bloud was spilde,
Whereof I had a share ; and when I call
To minde those heroes' lamentable falle,
(Riche, Brette, Conway, [f] and the rest, whose bones
Wante even a monument of marble stones,)
My soule wastes into sighes, my troubled braines
To teares, but that a manly hearte disdaines

---

[a] " Over " in margin.                    [b] " That the foe landed," Sloane MS.

[c] The Sloane MS. reads—

> "They durst not, but we hear they did descrie
> A heedlesse duke, a headlesse companie,
> But oh ! what men or angels can devise
> To excuse, &c."

[d] " Bruite " in margin; "taunts " in Sloane MS.

[e] " coble vile," in Mr. Fairholt's version.

[f] Sir Alexander Brett, sir Charles Rich, and sir Edward Conway were among the sufferers.   (Court and Times of Charles I. vol. i. p. 284.)

Such female follies, but I hope to see
Those Worthies' deathes, proud France, revengde in thee.
But is the duke come safelie home againe,
Triumphing o're his conquered countrymen,
As if such valiant leaders' mournfull slaughter
Were but a subjecte for such cowarde's laughter?
Leave upstarte greatnes, ere it be too late;
Submitte thy selfe, be governde by the State;
For if but one yeere more thou lorde it thus,
Thou'lt drawe confusion on thy selfe and us.
Stay, stay at Courte, and nowe at Tennis play,
Measure French galliardes, or goe kill a greye.
Venus' pavilions doe become the beste,
Periwigs with helmets use not to be preste.
To overcome Spaine, winne Cales, [a] and conquer France,
Requires a soldier's marche, no courtier's dance.
Let valiant, skillfull Generalles be chose
That dare in bloud confront theire proudest foes;
Then there's some hope we may recover our losses,
And make our enemies to rue our crosses.
Three things have lost our honor, all surmise—
Thy trecherie, neglecte, and cowardise.

These verses came forthe, as I did heare, soone after the returne from Rees; in which, whether any more be sette downe then vulgar rumor, which is often lying, I knowe not; but this I knowe, that those which are in esteeme and greatest favour with princes are most subjecte to slander of tongues, the vulgar delighting herein, who judge of all things by events, not by discretion. At the first reporte of this voyage, they could speake well.

Sir William Withepoll, his fowle facte. At the beginning of this yeere's spring, one [b] Wright, a lieftenant (some say captaine) and [b] Maddeson, an ancient

A second is one chosen to helpe in a quarrel. bearer, that belonged to soldiers billeted at Woodbridge, were drawne into a challenge with a brother of sir William Wittipoll, and one [b] Timperley, his second, both papists; the other protestants, of which Maddeson was the second; which combate, by

[a] Cadiz.     [b] Blank in MS.

Timperley's subtiltye, was appointed at the horse-race post by Cleye [a] in Swafham heathes, where, he said, they were all vnknowne (yet at Oxborough [b] neere hand he was well knowne); for which they mette at Swafham, a day or two before; but it seemeth Maddeson, comming to the Crowne there, and finding Timperley (a day before the combate day), tould him that he heard Mr. Wittipoll would put on a fenced coate, wherefore his maister should fight in his shirte.   Timperley replied in flowting manner that he would then get coulde, whereupon a quarrell beganne, wherein Timperley was dangerously wounded, so that had he not had there a chirurgian brought with him, he had hardly escaped.   After this, some wordes of Wittipoll and his cowardise being spread abroad in Suffolk, it seemeth sir William tooke parte; and one day, not long before the ende of the session of parliament, came with his brother, and all his company of trained men, to Martlesham [c] heath, not farre from Woodbridge, where Wright and Maddeson, with theire company of 28 men or there about, mette them, the soldiers being lefte on the other side the bridge, and they, Wright and Maddeson, going over to sir William and his brother, who were gone aside from theire men, the conclusion was sir William and his brother did cowardly pistoll both Wright and Maddeson, whereat there fell some shotte betweene the two companies, and one on Ipswich side had his braines shotte out behinde the head, by one of his owne company that stood behinde him.   Sir William and his company marched to Ipswich, and there caused all the belles (where they could prevaile) to be rung; the next day he rode to London, and submitted himselfe to the councell, and tould his owne tale; but being imprisoned in the King's Bench, and there at the King's Benche barre to be tried— we heare July 28, that he and his keeper are fledde. [d]

*Sir William Wittipoll.*

*Not true.*

The facte no doubte was fowle.   His meanes, of his owne and his

[a] Cockley-Cley, four miles from Swaffham.
[b] Parish in Greenhoe hundred, co. Norfolk.
[c] Parish in the hundred of Carleford, co. Suffolk.
[d] See Court and Times of Charles I. vol. i. pp. 413, 414.

wives, were 6000 yeerly. His adversaries greate, and Maddeson father a man of 12 score annuatim, with 1,000*li.* in his purse, an resolute withall; so that no ransome would be had, but he woul sue an appeale, &c.

Twelve men of a jury of life and death were fined by Judg Harvie, x*li.* eche man, which he promised that they should surely pay

They passed upon one Diglets, an horseleach or farrier and gunne apperteining to sir H. Bedingfield at Oxborough, whom witnesse (*ut dicitur*) proved to have threatned the fyring of a widdowe house, to have had fyer in a potshearde abroade in the night, abou an houre before the house was fyred, that the potshearde was th next day found neere the house burned, &c. A second was on proved to have ij. wives. A third a tayler, that confessed that h had his shieres in his hands, and that unfortunately his wife wa killed; now the pointe of the shieres were sticked in hir necke under or behinde the eare. A fowerth was a yong fellowe, a smith that having ij. wenches with child, carryed one away (to marry he as he said) in the night, and in a close about Hales greene put he into an oulde well, neere 40 foote deepe, where she continued 4 daye at the least, and yet at the last being pulled out, was recovered, an her child saved, she having litle hurte, but with the noysomnes o the place, among toades and newtes, &c., the bottome being drie He was accused for conspiring her death. All these they found no guilty. The judge tould them that they had brought murther o themselves, and other fowle felonyes, besides the wounding of their consciences in breaking theire oathe.

This spring and summer, even untill mid July, wondrous coul and wette, with many frostes, which by reason of the wett di litle hurte at Weeting.[b]

---

[a] Parish in the hundred of Clavering, co. Norfolk.
[b] Weeting, a parish in Norfolk, where the writer's father was rector of the church All Saints.

About this time, a greate navy againe going forthe, some say 80 <sup>August 1.</sup> English and 60 Scottish shippes. God blesse us! <sub>A navy.</sub>

The reporte is, that the duke being at Portesmouth, readie to goe out with this navy, one lieftenant Felton, whose captaine's place was void in the Low countreyes, came to the duke on Fryday, <sub>At Rees.</sub> August 22, to begge the captaine's place; the duke tould him he would demurre; the next day he commeth againe with a petition <sub>grant.</sub> drawne, and what answere he had is uncertaine; but (*ut dicitur*) he presently drewe out his ponyard and stabde him to the hearte. The duke would have drawne his sword, but fayled, and uttering <sub>Duke slaine.</sub> these wordes, " What villaine gave me this blowe?" spake no more, <sub>Some say he</sub> but died within two houres. It is said Felton avowed the facte, and <sub>swore and<br>cursed much.</sub> said he had done God, the king, and country, good service, for he, the duke, wold have undone England if he had gone this voyage. Thus the reporte. The certainty of this is thus. Upon Saturday, <sub>Aug. 23.</sub> Aug. 23, in the morning, newes came to Portsmouth of Rochell, <sub>As said Mr.</sub> that it was relieved, whereupon the duke being at breakfast with <sub>Eade from<br>Cambridge, yet</sub> the earl of Holland and Wat. Montague, the duke his favorite, <sub>he might be<br>deceived.</sub> did determine when breakfast was ended to goe to the King, who lay within 4 miles, newly recovered of the poxe. In the meane time, navy captaines, lieftenants, and others, assembled into the duke's lodgings, expecting his comming forth, to knowe the certainty of the newes; and as the duke came amongst them, going through the chamber where they were, one Felton, either a captaine or lieftenant, to whom the duke did denie some place that he thought was his right, with a stiletto stroke the duke in to the lefte side, and <sub>A knife.</sub> lefte the weapon there. The duke only gave a shrike, and fell downe presently. The company were busie about the duke, to see if he could be holpen, and at length enquired after the agent, who not being gone, shewed himselfe, and avowed the facte, saying he had done God and his country good service.

September 2. This I received, either as a copie of words uttered <sub>Sept. 2.</sub> by the agent, or of some writing found about him, or both:—

" Let no man commend me for what I have done, but rather dis-commend themselves; for if that God, for theire sinnes, had not taken away theire harte, this man could not have continued thus long amongst us.

" I shall ever accompt him very base, and not worthy the name of a soldier, who will not be readie to sacrifice his life, for the glory of God, the honour of the king, and good of the country.

" JOHN FELTON."[a]

About September 3, I had related to me this foolish and dan-gerous rime, fruite of an after witte—

J. F. had it of
Rich. Garn.

> J. and C.[b] have done what they can,
> And G.[c] must die as did Doctor Lambe.[d]

GEORGIUS DUX BUCKINGAMIE.
MDCXVVVIII.

Received
Sept. 16, from
Will. Crosse.

> Læto jam sæclo tandem sol protulit annum—1628.
> Noni ne videat quæsumus, Alme, diem.

> Thy numerous name with this yeere will agree,
> But twenty-nine God graunt thou never see ! [e]

Newes from
Sturbridge.

Since the duke's death, the Lord Willoughby is sent forth as generall and commander with the navy.[f]

---

[a] This contains the sense, but not the words, of Felton's paper. See the fac-simile engraved in C. J. Smith's " Historical and Literary Curiosities," 1840, 4to., and the words in the Gentleman's Magazine, N. S. xxiv. 141. The original, formerly in the Upcott collection, is now missing.

[b] For James and Charles.            [c] George.

[d] Rushworth, pt. i. p. 618, gives it somewhat differently, but the version of the MS. is probably the correct one—

> Let Charles and George do what they can,
> The duke shall die like Doctor Lamb.

[e] This distich was said in a copy in Ashmolean MS. XXXVIII. p. 25, to have been written by John Marston, several months before the murder of the duke. Mr. Fairholt's Intro-duction to " Poems, &c." p. xvi.

[f] He was previously vice-admiral.

A LETTER FROM ONE OF THE HIGHAMS.

I knowe that the newes of the strangest disaster that ever was done by an Englishman upon the person of so great a man, is by this time spredde farre and wide, though acted but yesterday, about eight in the morne. The day before, being the 22nd of August, a sayler that had affronted the duke a seventhnight before, was by a martiall courte condemned to die; after which (he being caried to our prison by myselfe with our whole guard) the saylers in greate multitudes drewe together with cudgels and stones, and assayed with great fury to take him from us, insomuch that there fell out a greate muteny amongst us, that I was enforced to let fly my muskets, though not with intente to kill (because I had no order); but we received blowes with stones and cudgels, and had much to doe to keepe the prisoner. But the captaines of the fleete came up to us, and drewe upon the saylers with greate fury, and banged and slashed them dangerously, by which time the duke himselfe, with a great company on horsebacke, came fresh upon them too; where there was 200 swordes drawen, and where the duke behaved himselfe very nobly and bravely, and drewe [a] all the saylers on the porte pointe, and made them all fly on shipborde, wherein many were dangerously hurte and two killed outright. He retired within the towne againe; and himselfe in person sawe the first mutinere carried with a guarde to the gibbet, where he was hanged by the handes of another mutinous sayler, who himselfe was saved for that good office. The other had not dyed if they had not then mutined, for the Dutches had begged his life. Now the next morne, which was Saturday the 23, there came one Jo. Felton (a gentleman borne neere to Sudbury in Suffolk), to towne, who laye but three miles from towne the night before, in his journey from London. So soone as he came, he repayred to the duke's lodging, where I had a

[a] " drave " in margin.

strong guarde; he went unknowne amongst many, and yet well knowne amongst many (as having beene a liefetenant in the army), into the hall. The duke having received that morning certaine newes that Rochell was relieved, was very jocant and well pleased; and addressed himselfe with all speed to carry newes thereof to the King. Many of his company being ready on horsebacke, and himselfe comming out of the parlour, colonell Fryer mette him and saluted him; the duke also, according to his courteous manner, saluted him, and lifting himselfe up, while colonell Fryer still stouped, this Felton with a knife reached over the colonel's shoulder, and stabbed the duke above the lefte pappe, cleane through a ribbe. The duke, pulling the knife himselfe out, cryed with a greate oathe, " Traytor, thou hast killed me," and drewe his sworde halfe out, and so fell downe and never spake worde more. When with a showting shrike every body withdrewe, and none knewe who killed him, Felton, who might have escaped, offered himselfe, saying, " I am the man; why doe you not kill me?" who then had much to doe to be saved. But then the wofull spectacles in every roome of the house, with the dutches and other ladies, lords, knights, and gentlemen's direfull lamentings, wringings, with shrikes and cryes, what hearte could endure? The villaine, in respect of my office, was presently committed to me; and I carryed him with my guard to God's House, where three of the privy councell came to take his examination, which done, I brought him to our prison, where he remaines with a guard upon him. He is a very bould resolute young man, and doth not repent his facte, as perswading himselfe that he hath done good service to the king, state, and country.[a]

<hr />

[a] Other accounts of the duke of Buckingham's assassination will be found in his Life by Sir Henry Wotton, in Lord Clarendon's History, in the Memoirs of Sir Simonds Dewes, and in a letter of Sir Dudley Carleton to the Queen, in Ellis's Orig. Letters, First Series, iii. 137. See also the Gentleman's Magazine for August 1845.

## AN EPITAPH.[a]

" I that my country did betray,
　Undidde the King who let me sway
　His scepter as I pleased, brought downe
　The glory of the English crowne,
　The courtiers' bane, the countries hate,
　An agent for the Spanish state;
　The papists' frende, the gospel's foe,
　The church and kingdome's overthrowe,
　Here an odious carkase dwell,
　Untill my soule returne from hell;
　With Judas then I shall inherit
　Such portion as all traytors merit.
　If heaven admitte of treason, pride, and luste,
　Expecte my spotted soule among the juste.

　Some say the duke was gracious, vertuous, good,
　And Felton basely did to spill his bloud;
　If so, what did he doe amisse,
　In sending him the sooner to his blisse?
　Pale death seemes pleasing to a good man's eye,
　And only badde men are afrayde to die.
　If that he lefte this kingdome to possesse a better,
　Why then hath Felton made the duke his debtor. [c]

　Awake, sadde Britaine, and advance at last
　Thy drooping heade; let all thy sorrowes past
　Be drownde and sunke with theire owne teares, and nowe
　O'relooke thy foes with a triumphant browe.

Received these,
Sept. 16,
T. Jen.[b]

---

[a] This epitaph is printed, almost verbatim, in Mr. Fairholt's " Poems on the Duke of Buckingham," p. 51, from Ashmole MS. XXXVIII. art. 18.　At the end of the verses in that MS. occur the words, "Finis, Jo. Heape."　" We are thus supplied," writes Mr. Fairholt, " with the name of the author of one of the bitterest rhymes of the series brought forth on this remarkable event."

[b] Query, Thomas Jenner, a London printer of the period.

[c] This and the following lines are printed with slight variations from Sloane MS. 603, in pp. 66, 67 of Mr. Fairholt's collection.

Thy foe, Spaine's agent, Holland's bane, Rome's frend,
By a victorious hand receivde his ende.
Live ever Felton, thou hast turnde to dust
Treason, ambition, murther, pride, and lust."

Hence maye be seene how that the greatest are subject to th
scorne of witte.  Light scoffing wittes, not apte to deeper reache
can rime upon any the most vulgar surmises, and will not faile t
shewe themselves, though charity and true wisedome forbidde.  C
this duke, my prayer hath alwaies beene, if he were so bad as th
vulgar counted him, that God would discover him; but if not, tha
God would mainteine his honour if he were faithfull.  And, not
withstanding all these things, I should have beene free from al
harder censure of him, but that the parliament did so oppose him
The wise will never be rashly uncharitable; yet time may tell u
what we may safely thinke.

To have alwaies the best conceite and opinion of men's actions i
truly helde in matters of state amongst wise statesmen very dan
gerous.  In greatest trust is often greatest treason.

Rochell re-
lieved.
False.

The newes about September 29 was, that my lord Willoughby
who by a late honour is earl of Linsey, hath with our navy an
English forces relieved Rochell, and raised the siege both at sea an
land, &c.  Not so then.[a]

September.
Lord Brooke
slaine.

About the beginning of September, came certain newes of th
death of sir Fulke Grevill, lord Brooke, of Beauchamp's Courte i
Warwickshire, aged about eighty, who had beene a privy councello
in queen Elizabeth and king James his time.  The manner wa
thus: a servant, upon some discontente about maintenance, did i
his privy chamber stabbe him about the brest with a knife, but b
some rib mist his aime, and then stabbed him in the belly.  Th
lord crying out, he ranne into the next roome and locked the dor
and then ranne upon his owne rapier against the wall; but fayling, h

---

[a] See Court and Times of Charles I. vol. i. p. 405.

tooke the former knife that lay by his dead maister, and stabbed himselfe therwith, and so died ere any could breake in.

Newes in October, that, ere Bartholomewe fayer was done, there August. was a picture sold (to which much running), wherein was drawen a naked young woman, and besides her, or before her, one riding on The D. the backe of an ougly ould woman, and thus under it:

> " All you that will goe with me,
> I'le carry you to yᵉ naked ile of Re."

It was then tould us by a Londoner, J. Normansell, that at the time of the duke's funerall the soldiers or companies of London were present; and, being by command to traile theire pikes and beate dolefully for the duke, they contrarily did beate up amaine with courage, and shouldered theire pikes. The earle of Dorset, they say, found faulte, but could not tell how to helpe it. The duke's body embalmde, and wrapped in leade, is (*ut dicitur*) set aside, for the deane of Westminster would not let it be buried there, &c.

A booke is come forth of Doctor Lambe.

October 29, I had a coranto at Norwich, wherein was a liste of October. the names of fifty-two shippes, Rochelers and English, that joyned with our navy at Plimmouth; where I was also tould, that a former coranto had a liste of the navy from Portsmouth (as was remembred) of 120 ships; eight or twelve have gone since with victuals; all make nine score.

It was reported that the dole for the duke was farthings; and an Older than the ould rime was rehearsed: duke's death.

> " Brasse farthings in charity are given to the pore,
> When all the gold pieces are spent on a whore."

Thus foully will the vulgar disgrace him whose greatenes they hate.

October 30. Mr. Sutton, of Eriswell,ᵃ as he said, was at Thetford, Rochell yielded. and there preached; where he heard of a letter sent to sir Anthony Quere?

---

ᵃ A parish in the north of Suffolk.

Sir George Gor-
ing, now a
baron.

Newes of Ro-
chell.

Plantation in
Nova Francia
destroyed.   At
Canada rather.

November.

Winkfield from the lord Goring, usher to the queene, wherein it
was said that Rochell was yeelded up to the king of France, with
conditions hard enough, said many.

November 16. Newes from sir Drugh Drewry, that it was
yeelded to the king of France upon condition to pay 300,000
crownes to our king, promised at the marriage; and they must
receive a garrison of the king's, and so they shall have theire liberty
for religion. That this was offered by the king because he is
enforced to diverte his warres to the Valtolin, where Spaine
encrocheth.

At the same time the newes was, that our men did watche the
lading of the French at Nova Francia; and when they were prepared of all theire lading, very rich for France, then they tooke all
theire shippes and victualls; moreover, that they tooke in all theire
men least they should perish, and brought them home, landing them
in Holland, from whence they might goe home.

It is thought by diverse that the duke, having his duchesse at
Portsmouth, meante on the suddaine to have carried her on shipborde at their hoisting of saile, and to have carried all to Venice,
and there to have sold all the ships and goodes, and then to have
provided for himselfe there.

The former newes for Nova Francia was thus, as is reported:
One captain Kirke, conducting some English soldiers through
France, received fowle discurtesies of the French, and being come
home, he vowed to be revenged; of which the French hearing, sent
five ships of warre for defense of theire plantation in America; for
Kirke, by helpe of a rich father in London and some partners in the
adventure, prepared two ships and a pinnace. When he was set
out, a storme tooke them, and parted him from his other ship and
pinnace; the storme also parted the French (*ut dicitur*), so that the
next day he light upon one of them and tooke it; and then the
next day after fell upon his ship and pinnace, with all which he
went on; tooke the French ships in the harbour, burnte the towne,

pillaged all, brought away some eighty pieces of brasse ordonance, and drowned the rest of iron; being come home, he went to the king, who knighted him, and gave him his share, so that the adventure was whole to themselves.[a]  He delivered a prince that the French had taken in the country, who by two Jesuites was put to torment by a suite of apparell whose linings were full of prickes. The Jesuites in the comming home were put to tast of the same sawce.  This prince was diverse dayes together, in the beginning of Michaelmas terme, at the Royall Exchange to be seene.

At this time, in Nov., a constant reporte of many millions of Spanish treasure, taken by the Hollander, as it came home from the West Indies with many ships.  *Spanish treasure taken. True.*

November 20, our fleete was come home or neere it, with some losse of a fewe small ships; Rochell being delivered up to theire owne king.  *Our fleet returned, Rochel yeelded.*

About this time, an East India ship returned home, with exceeding much wealth; and, being come to the Downes in Kent, many adventurers and theire wives went into her, to see her, and make merry; but a storme arose, and drave her (so that the cables brake) unto the coast of Holland; and about Texel roade she was lost, and all that was in her, adventurers, theire wives, and frends, and all.  *East India ship lost at home.*

November 28, the last day of the terme, John Felton, that had killed the duke, was arraigned, by 8 in the morning, at the King's Bench barre, and confessed the facte; being condemned to be hanged, which was executed the next day at Tiburne: and so was carried *(ut dicitur)* to be hanged in chaines.  All the blame for Rochell is layd upon the duke, for if viscount Fielding had not wanted commission, he had prevented the blocking up of the haven that now hindered us.  *Felton executed.*

This last Michael[mas] terme many were fined and sore punished.  *December.*

---

[a] This adventure was near Canada and Newfoundland.  See Court and Times of Charles I. vol. i. pp. 405, 409, 417.

One scholler for speaking wordes against the King.   Another for saying that Felton would have hired him to kill the duke, and that many
noble men were in the conspiracy.   Felton said he knewe not the
man, nor the man him; and for tryall the man was to be brought
where Felton was, and another man put in place; he saluted him by
the name of Mr. Felton, and when Felton came, he tooke no knowledge of him.

Doctor Ravens, a physitian in Cambridge, rich, who had had ij. rich
wives, presumed to get into the chamber of a widowe, an alderman's
daughter, worth 20,000*li.*, and put his legge into the bedde: she
asked who was there; he answered "Doctor Ravens;" she cryed
out, and company came in.   Thus the tale is told.   He was fined
500 pound, besides imprisonment and other disgrace.   The widowe's
action against him is yet to come.[a]

Proclamations ij.   I sawe at Thetford, December 20: 1. having
relation to a statute, made in the ende of king James's reigne, for
the security of the subjecte in his tenure of lands questioned
under pretence of concealement, assuring the tenure where the king
had made no claim within 60 yeeres: and nowe, for those lands not
secured by that statute, and for defective patents and grantes, &c.,
the king hath appointed commissioners, with whom if any will compound, theire estates shall be secured for ever.[b]   The other proclamation was for the apprehending of one Richard Smith, a perilous
seducing Seminary, and against all such as should be his abbettors or
harbourers.[c]

The Palsgrave's eldest sonne was drowned (Henry), the boate
wherein he was being cast away not farre from Amsterdam.   The
Palsgrave himselfe, as some say, was the only man that was saved.

---

[a]   See Court and Times of Charles I., vol. i. pp. 436-437, 443.   The young widow had two
other suitors, sir Sackville Crow and sir John Finch : the wits of the day said that of her
three birds, Finch, Crow, and Raven, the Raven had the worst of it.

[b]   Date, 6th December, 1628, Fœdera, vol. viii. pt. iii. pp. 5, 6.

[c]   Date, 11th December, 1628, Fœdera, vol. viii. pt. ii. p. 6.   See note, p. 39.

Two noble men were also drowned (as is reported), and the occasion of theire being in a boate was to see the greate prise lately taken by the Hollanders, of the Spanish treasure.    It is too certaine that Henry, the eldest sonne, is drowned.

The parliament againe assembled.[a]                                    Parliament.

The newes was at London, in Hillary term, that the upper house of Parliament did much distaste the bishop of London, for that he had throwne downe a booke of articles at his first comming in.    The cause might be this: Doctor Laud, bishop of London, as is likely accompanied with some others, had some while before this session of parliament gotten the King to ratifie the Articles of religion 1562, with a charge that no man should teach contrary, &c., by which it may be the bishop thought to stay the parliament's intermeddling with Arminianisme and matters of religion, for reformation and setling whereof he sawe there was an intendment; and high time too, but he prevailed not; for Arminians of note, bishops and others, have beene convented, and will be so dealt with as God shall permitte.

*Perhaps not true.  See †belowe.*

" Babell not Bethel[c] " was now printed.    Also " God no Impostor;"   Barret's   Recantation;   and   " Novem  Positiones;"  &c. or Articles of Lambeth, printed together.[d]

*Page 64. †b*

The newes was, February 27, that upon an intendment to censure Mr. Cosen,[e] the King caused the parliament to stay theire sitting

*Not true.*

---

[a] His Majesty's speech at Whitehall, Jan. 24th, 1628-9, and Mr. Rous's speech on the 26th of the same January, are omitted here, as printed in Rushworth.

[b] Page 38 *infra.*

[c] "Babel not Bethel, *i.e.* the Church of Rome no true visible Church of Christ; being an Answer to Hugh Cholmeley's Challenge, and Robert Butterfield's Maschill." By Hen. Burton, 4to. Lond. 1628.

[d] By William Prynne, 4to. Lond. 1629.    "Barrett's Recantation " of 1595 was translated by him, and published with the " Novem positiones, or Lambeth articles," and other controversial tracts of the period.

[e] Dr. John Cosins, afterwards Bishop of Durham, published " A collection of Private Directions in the Practice of the Ancient Churches, called The Hours of Prayer," 8vo.

untill March 2. It is not true; but rather it is thought that th
house rose to demurre about some busines propounded by the King
whereupon he also demurred untill March 2, forbidding them to s
untill then: some say that the King, having stayed men's goods fo
poundage, the cause was tryed, and it passed for the King, the record
whereof some would have had burnt, some not, &c.

Doctor Laud, bishop of London, they say, whereas the King ha
selected certaine councellors to sitte and consulte to prepare for th
parliament, did forestall them by presenting a copie of Articles, to b
followed if approved; for which sir Edward Cooke blamed hi
sharpely, as a young councellor; and so did the earl of Pembrooke
telling the bishop that his packe was broken.

**Parliament dissolved.** This parliament was dissolved, March 2, by proclamation.[a]  Se
the booke of the King's declaration, made to his subjects, of the cause
why he dissolved it.

**1629.** In Aprill, I received a copy of this prognostication, sent abroad,
believe, to busy the heades of the vulgar, in this troublesome time
and to hinder theire talke of state matters.  " A prognostication sen
to his Imperiall Majestie and the illustrious Prince of Saxonie. 1629
Sunne in Libra, and all the planets about her prognosticate horribl
**Prognostication.** things; tempests by meeting of the 4 windes; earthquakes that shal
cause many for feare to die; trees and buildings shall be cast downe
especially neere waters; horrible eclipses; a bloudy rain-bowe; strang
bloudy warres; the emperor and his subjects are moved to repentance
and he to withdrawe himselfe into some convenient place, with pro
vision for xxx dayes.  Approved by Arinarguers Spanish an
Grecian astrologers.

May 28. Greate assembly of men of warre.

June 11. Three greate princes shall die.

London, 1627 ; to which Prynne replyed in a pamphlet entitled " A brief Survey and Cen
sure of Mr. Cozens his cousening devotions, proving them to be merely Popish."   4t
London, 1628.

[a] Fœdera, vol. viii. pt. iii. p. 2.

12. A lord shall atteine to great dignity and honor.

18. A great wind.

19. A banished prince shall returne to his owne country and receive his former dignity.

28. Greate intollerable heate.

August 14. Greate preparation for warre, by sea and land.

17. Greate effusion of bloud.

18. Halfe the world shall be drowned.

20. Busines of greate importance sent from many places."

The same time I sawe upon a poste in the sadler's shoppe at Watton a proclamation, thus:—

" By the King.—A proclamation for the calling in and suppressing of two sermons preached and printed by doctor Manwairing, doctor in divinity, entituled 'Religion and Allegiance.'" [b]

About this time was printed a like proclamation for suppressing of " *Appello Cæsarem*," made by Richard Montague, then Batchelor of Divinity, nowe Bishop of Chichester,[c] &c.   This I sawe about March last, in the handes of Mr. Osbert Pratte senior.   Doctor White, now Bishop of Norwich, did at Paul's crosse recante his approbation of that booke (*ut dicitur*). {Montague's Appeal to Cæsar suppressed.}

Captaine Kirke goeth out with 10 ships, to plant at the Canada in      degrees north, where he displanted the French before.

William Leader tould me, April 4, that he lately heard one of the lord keeper's gentlemen reporte that a bishop should say of another bishop thus:—" If I had authority, that bishop should be set on the pillory thrice, with his faults written about him, and then should be imprisoned, and after imprisonment should be brought forth and burnte at a stake."

Newes that Mr. Burton, who wrote "Babell not Bethell," and

---

[a] A parish in the hundred of Wayland, co. Norfolk.

[b] Printed in the Fœdera, vol. viii. pt. ii. p. 264 ; dated June 24th, 1628.

[c] It bears date 17th January, 1629.   Fœdera, vol. viii. pt. iii. p. 20.

[d] Blank in MS.

Page 61 †ᵃ
*untrue.*ᶜ

Mr. Prin, who printed " God no Impostor,"ᵇ Barret's Recantation
and Lambeth Articles (as you may see 2 leaves backward), were both
imprisoned.   Doubtfull.

### A Copie of a Letter sent from the Devill to the Pope.

To the most pious, vertuous, and religious Primate of all Christendome,
Urban 8, now Pope of Rome, and Vicegerent here upon earth, Lucifer, God
of the Gehenna, King of Tartarus, Prince of Abyssus, Commander of the Infernall Furies, sendeth greeting.

Most reverend and deere sonne, whose holines I reverence, whose person I
adore, whose policie I wonder at, I cannot but applaud, extoll, and commende
thee, my deere sonne, for thy extraordinary greate meanes, costes, and charges
in the preparation of so great forces against the Rebellious heretikes from the
Roman Catholike religion, I meane the British, Irish, Danish, and Flemish
heretikes ; the particulars of which course I have in writing, and I heare say
likewise that they are published to the whole world.   Therefore followe it
nowe with all celeritie and expedition.   Now be the dayes to conquer; nowe
is the time to strike.   God hath forsaken them ; theire land is impoverished,
theire ships tattered ; theire state is weakened ; theire parliament is ended
and nothing amended ; the nobles disquieted ; theire gentry discouraged ; the
Commons discontented ; and the whole kingdome divided ; and the Roman
Catholikes in England gasping and gaping for your arrivall.   Therefore strike
nowe, or else for ever hereafter hold thine hand.   By this meanes, thou mai'ste
root out and extirpate all malitious, turbulent, and evill affected spirits against
Else there is not
five. the sea of Rome.   There are but 5 nations thou needest to feare in the world ;
the king of greate Britaine, the king of Denmarke, *(the king of Sweden,*ᶜ*)* the
Palsgrave, falsly usurping the title of king of Bohemia, and the Rebellious
Hollanders.   But what are those against thee, but so many molehilles to
mountaines ; and no more, in our handes, then a lambe in the pawes of a lyon?
Yet it were not amisse to practise some deadly stratagem, by poulder or
poyson, by my servants the Seminaries and Jesuites, especially upon the king of
greate Brittaine and the Palsgrave's children (King Henry V.'s faces and
Queene Elizabeth's hearty apes); for if these be not cut of in the blossomes,
but continue to be ripe fruite, it is to be feared they will doe much harme.

ᵃ Inserted afterwards.

ᵇ " God no Impostor nor Deluder ; or, an Answer to a Popish and Arminian Cavil, in
Defence of Free-will and Universal Grace."   4to.   London, 1630.

ᶜ Added afterwards.

And I heare say that my servant Spinola hath received my Sacraments, and sworne to St. James, by his Agnus Dei, that he would spend his best bloud in England, against the Revolters from the Romish Church, which I, cruell fortune, and fate conspire so to effecte. It is my desire that his hearte may be baked in a pastie, and sent to the nunnes of St. Lucas; his bones may be buried in the Cathedrall Church of Civill, and his stones to be conveyed to my handmaide the Archdutches, [a] for a token of his love. And so, my deere sonne, I bidde the farewell.

It was tould us that one Mr. Fountaine, a French Catholike, who hath married Mr. Drapier's sister of Eriswell, and was wonte to write him newes from London, wrote lately that he could have sent April 17. newes, but he feared his necke.

Diverse parliament men, to the number of 8 or more, as is said, were committed to prison, for contempt committed in the parliament house of Commons, of whom we may reade in the King's booke, declaring the causes of dissolving the last parliament. These men, as is said, or at least one of them was brought to be tried, but he refused all triall in this kind, except it were by parliament, because Easter terme. his offense was not a private man's offense, but publike, in the parliament house, &c.

The newes is that mariners are pressed to serve in the bringing over of the queene mother, the queene being with child. May 15, newes was that the queene was delivered of a young prince, borne Queene's deliverance. before the time. Not long since, was published a proclamation for Charles christened. the apprehending of Richard Smith, a Jesuite, who calleth himselfe the Bishop of Chalcedon.[b] Another prohibiting talke of parliaments Proclamation. &c.[c] About May 10, a proclamation for peace with France, concluded about April 14.[d]                                            Peace with France.

---

[a] Isabella Clara Eugenia, Infanta of Spain, widow of the Archduke Albert of Austria, and governor of the Spanish Netherlands.

[b] This second proclamation was dated 24th March, 1629. See Rushworth, pt. ii. vol. i. p. 13, where is an account of the Bishop of Chalcedon. See also the Discovery of the Jesuits at Clerkenwell, in the second volume of the Camden Miscellany.

[c] Fœdera, vol. viii. pt. iii. p. 36.          [d] Ibid. p. 39.

Ellis <sub>a</sub> and Hollis.

The protestation of the Commons in parliament.[b]

1. Whosoever shall bring in an innovation in religion, or countenance, seeke to extende, or introduce Popery or Arminianisme, or other opinions disagreeing from the true and orthodoxe profession of our Church, shall be reputed a capitall enemie to the kingdome and commonwealth.

2. Whosoever shall councell or advise the taking or levying of the subsides of the tonnage and poundage (not being granted by parliament), or shall be an actor or instrument therein, shall likewise be reputed an innovator in the government, and a capitall enemie to the kingdome and commonwealth.

3. If any merchant or person whatsoever shall voluntarily yeeld or pay the said subsides, tonnage, and poundage (not being granted by parliament), he shall likewise be reputed a betrayer of the liberties of England, and an enemie to the same.

Thus much was the speaker forced to utter at the dissolving of the parliament (or after the dissolving), while the dores were kept. See page 64 capite, where this takes place. *Hinc lachrymæ.*

Perhaps it should be Elliot and Hollis, page prior.

| Sir John Elliot. [c] | | | |
|---|---|---|---|
| Mr. Daniel [d] Hollis. | | | Sir Peter Haymonde [e] to the gatehouse. |
| Denzill Hollis. | to the Tower. | | Sir Miles Hobart to the Fleet. |
| Mr. Selden. | | | |
| Mr. Valentine. | | | Mr. Long, Mr. Strowde sent for. |
| Mr. Coriton. | | | |

These should have beene tried this Ester terme, but it was pleaded

---

a Sir John Eliot, see below.

b Rushworth, pt. i. p. 660.

c For the prosecution of Elliot, Hollis, and Valentine, see Rushworth, pt. i. pp. 683, 686.

d Denzil.

e Hayman. See Rushworth, pt. i. p. 661.

that the faulte was not as of private men, but done (if it were a faulte) in parliament, and otherwise then by parliament they would not be tryed; so they were sent backe.

It is most certaine that a crowe did often build in the top of Wil- Aprill.
ton [a] windmill, plying it late at night and early in the morning, when Crowe built in
the miller was absent.  She layd an egge there.  Her nest was layd a mill saile.
betweene the shrowdes in the toppe saile, and so much of the saile
cloth aloft as is usually with the wind driven out like a poke.

A proclamation at Bury for peace with France, declaring that the
ould amitie betweene the two kingdomes is renued, [b] pag. pr.  A Proclamation
proclamation prohibiting all transportation of corne to forreine partes,[c] for stay of corn.
though the prises fall within the statute liberty.  The reasons are May 18.
disliked at the buyers' hands, who thinke the publishing doth much
hurte.  2 reasons are rendred of this restrainte:—1. That the un-
reasonable weather hath caused that the present shewe on the ground
promiseth no plenty.  2. That kingdomes formerly wont to helpe
in time of dearth are not like now to doe so, &c.  Wherefore, to prevent extremity, the proclamation published.

One Maud grievously censured, for saying that the King had gone Maud censured.
to masse.

Sir William Withipoll (turne over this leafe) hath got his pardon,
and is at liberty.

The Hollanders doe besiege Hertogenbusse, the Bussy, as 'tis
usually called.

Sir William Withipoll and his brother, as it seemeth, were tried Sir William
and found guilty of manslaughter, and Sir William is againe endited Withipoll.  See
of accessory to the facte of his brother.  See the story 45. [d]          page 45.
                                                                        May.

About the last weeke in July fell out a grievous stirre in London, July.
neere the Temple, begunne by an arrest of a captaine (*ut dicitur*), A riot in Lon-
                                                                        don.

---

[a] Parish in the hundred of Grimshoe, co. Norfolk.

[b] Fœdera, vol. viii. pt. iii. p. 39, date 10th May, 1629.

[c] Ibid., p. 37, date 2nd May.

[d] Page 45 in MS.  See p. 22 *supra*.

and continuing many houres and one whole night, so that the Lord
Mayor and armed soldiers came.   Many were hurte, by brickebats
and such like, and 8 or 9 slaine by sword and shotte; some continued after 4 proclamations for departure; ij. young Ree captaines
Stanford and Ashton, were hanged.   Stanford had beene the duke'
man.[a]

August 6.  I had these verses delivered me.[b]

> The wisest King did wonder when he spied
> The noble[c] marche on foote, and [d] vassals ride.
> His Majestie may wonder now to see
> Some that will needes be King, as well as he,
> A rude presage of danger to this land,
> Where lowers strive to gette the upper hand,
> When Prince and Peeres to Pesants must obey,
> When lay-men to theire teachers teache the way:
> When Prin[e] and Prim and Jordan must divine,
> What lawe hath orthodox[f] and what divine.
> Good brother Baracke,[g] elder of Amsterdam,
> Shutte up at home your wilde Arminian ramme,
> If here he come, these men will cut his throate,
> Blessed Beucanian[h] sings them a sweeter note,
> And teaches howe to kirbe the power of Kings,
> And sheweth how to clip the Eagle's wings.

---

[a] This incident is recorded in Rushworth, with a proclamation for the arrest of the delin-
quents, under the year 1630.   See pt. ii. vol. i. p. 80.   The proclamation appears in the
Fœdera, vol. viii. pt. iii. p. 57, under the true date, 12th July, 1629.

[b] A copy in Sloane MS. 826, f. 152, is headed "Verses supposed to bee made by Dr
Corbet, Bishop of Oxford, against the opposing the Duke in Parliament, 1628," and is
followed by "An Answer to the same, lyne for lyne."

[c] "Nobles," Sloane MS.

[d] "their," Sloane MS.

[e] "Prym," Sloane MS. for Pym.

[f] "define What lords are hetrodox," Sloane MS.

[g] "Brough," Sloane MS.; but under neither name is there any work on the subject in
question.   Query, Is the reference to William Barclay's tract "De regno et regali potestate,
adversus *Buchananum*, Brutum et reliquos Monarchomachos."   12mo. Hanover, 1617.

[h] "Buchanan."   Probably referring to George Buchanan's treatise "De Jure Regni,"
in which the argument tends to prove the right of subjects to rebel against oppression.

It is a Puritan[a] that must set all right,
Then shall the Gospell shine as Phœbus bright,
Our Consistorian fabricke is the thing
We must set up, in spight of Church and King.
Against the Papists we have got the day,
Blinde Bishops only stand now in the way ;
But we will have a tricke to tame theire pride,
Tonnage and Poundage else shall be deny'de.

Doctor KERBIE, Bishop of Oxford.

*Corbet rather.* [b]

The Hollanders are upon a great voyage to the West Indiaes, with *August 1.* about 80 saile, and 30,000 men or above, to beleaguer the silver mines, &c.

The king of Denmarke hath, as some say, obteined an honour- *King of Denmark.* able peace with the emperor, having his townes restored. Certaine.[c]

About this time it beganne to be most certainly reported that, the *August 24.* Spanyard withdrawing his garrison-soldiers from Wesel, to aide about the Busse, as it is usuallie called, the prince,[d] with an armie from the leaguer, went (whether upon intelligence from the towne or no *Certain.* I know not) and tooke the towne of Wesel, where were 200 brasse *Wesel taken.* pieces, and wonderfull provision of poulder and victualls, for 50,000 for 3 months (*ut dicitur*), with other amunition.

The newes also is that the king of Sweden prevaileth both against the emperor and Poland.

Newes also of much shipping taken by Dunkerks on our coastes.

Newes of an island, 10 miles broad and 20 long, discovered by a *In the west* captaine sent out by the earle of Warwicke. *ocean.*

Newes from Sturbridge that the Bosche or Busse is yeelded to the Hollanders.

St. Hertogenbosche,[e] or the holy Busse, or Bosse-le-Duke (called *Busse yeelded.*

---

[a] " Paritie."                                 [b] Written afterwards.
[c] Written afterwards.                      [d] Henry Prince of Orange.
   [e] A comical mis-reading of the Dutch article Hets, generally contracted into 'Ts Hertogensbusche, by the French called Bois-le-Duc.

holy for the many monasteries therein) was yeelded to the States o
Henry Prince of Orange, &c. Sept. 4, 1629.   See the articles printed

Peace with
France.
In the latter end of September, an embassador here from France
and our King was sworne to the articles of peace.   The next day
after that, as it is said, the newes came to the King that the French
had cut the throates of 1400 English, at St. Christopher's Iland

Newes from St.
Christopher,
see page 72.
This newes held a while, but was crossed, and it was all [a] but this.
The French had taken some of our ships there, and by name one or
two of my lord of Warwicke's.[b]

The earle of Warwicke (they say) hath 8 shippes of warre, in
which he is often himselfe, taking many prises and enriching himselfe.

Dr. Lushing-
ton's sermon.
October 6.  I was at Mondeford[c] courte, where asking Mr. Tayler
what newes, he tould me that Mr. Barret had there showen a sermon
unprinted, lately preached at Whitehall before the King, upon
Mat. 28, 13, saying, " Say ye his disciples came by night," &c. by
Dr. Lushington, Oxfordiens.   I asked the drifte of it; he tould me
" witte."  I asked what was remarkeable; he said, first the beginning.   " What newes?  Every man askes what newes?  Every
man's religion is knowne by his newes; the Puritan talkes of
Bethlehem Gabor, &c."   Besides this, the doctor fell belike to
personate the chiefe priests and elders, in a florishing description of
our Saviour and his apostles, as impostors, &c. (a wicked witte), and
then comes to demande why the soldiers should say it, &c.   " Because," saith he (yet he mistooke his marke, see verse 14), " the
soldiers were audacious, and durst doe anything.   In those times,
(said he) the soldiers did depose and chuse emperors, yet the time
had beene when the priests did this.  But now peasants will doe all,
by prerogative of parliament, &c."

Raine.
This Michaelmas time, before and after, hath fallen wonderfull

[a] " untrue " is omitted.
[b] This was the truth of the affair.   See Court and Times of Charles I. vol. ii. pp. 27-8, 33.
[c] A parish in Grimshoe hundred, co. Norfolk.

store of raine, so that fences be drowned, fiering and stover loste, brakes at Weeting not to be got, because of the wette.    Corne riseth in price.

In October 1629, I having beene at Wickham Market,[a] at my cosen Games, with my wife and Anthony, in our returne, about Kesgrave,[b] betweene Woodbridge and Ipswich, I fell into the company of one Paine, a shopkeeper in Laxfield,[c] of whom, after much talke about Mr. Skinner and my ould acquaintance at Laxfield and Dennington,[d] I inquired of him if William Utting the toade-eater (of whom, see in my first long note-booke, covered with redder forrell, page 43, and in the notes of 1612) did not once keepe at Laxfield; he tould me yes, and said he had seene him eate a toade, nay two.    The man in whose house he kept went to him for his sake, and after salutation, tould him that a frend of his would give a groate to see him eate a toade (thus was the way to see it): he accepted the offer, and went and fetchte in, from under blockes, ij toades, and, rubbing of the earth (as in my other booke), he swallowed them downe, but presently he cast them up into his hands, and after some pawse, " Nay," saith he, " I will not loose my groate," so taking that which came up last (saith he) " thou wentst in first before and shalte so doe againe."    When both then were downe, his stomacke held them, and he had his groate.    This said Paine.    See my note-booke, what I saw, &c.

The newes was brought to Lees,[e] by the earle of Warwicke's coachman (who returned from the earle at London that day) that the earle was like to have a greate prise of 6 shippes of the silver fleete; who, being beaten by the Hollanders in the West Indies, yet able to stand out, at the comming in of a ship or ij of the earle's, upon the first broadside, yeelded.

William Utting, toade eater.

October 31. Earl of Warwick's prise.

---

[a] A parish in the hundred of Wilford, co. Suffolk.

[b] In the hundred of Carleford, co. Suffolk.

[c] In the hundred of Hoxne, co. Suffolk.

[d] Ibid.   Here was the family residence of the elder branch of the Rous family.

[e] Leigh priory, near Felstead, co. Essex, the seat of the earls of Warwick.

November.
Parliament prisoners offered release.

The newes is that the imprisonde parliament men were offered liberty if they would find suerties for theire good behaviour; which they refused. Some say one did yeeld. Others say he hearkened at the first, and then after, upon deliberation, was loath to urge his frends farre in a pointe that they were unwilling unto.

Lords confined or rather committed.

This Michaelmas terme, diverse lords were in trouble, for reading of a booke. It should seeme that there was a booke found in the duke's study, that had projects to get mony without a parliament, which booke a gentleman of Lincolne's Inne confuted, shewing the odiousnes and inconvenience of such courses. This confutation the lords confessed that they had reade, and cravde the King's mercy for that they had not revealed it.[a]

St. Christopher's.

It went for currant that the Spanyards had killed the French and Dutche at St. Christopher's and sent home our English; but nowe it is reported that, upon the landing of 2,000 men farre of in the Isle, our men left all to the spoile. The merchants loose, and the inhabitants are, its likely, driven to hard shiftes. The plantation likely to be left.

January.

The gentlemen that were prisoners for parliament busines were released, the last Michaelmas terme.

January.

Newes of Martin Southon's sonne, who hanged himselfe, this Christ-tide, at his father's dore.

January.

Newes of iij clothiers pistolld by three theeves, and the other three yeelding (6 in all); the theeves were taken in London.

January.

The newes is that the Spanyard must get all or loose all in Italy. The Jesuites and Pope fall from Spain to France. The Emperor is neere bankrupt.

Admirall.

The earle of Holland hath beene Admirall ever since Michaelmas terme; thus it is said.

Feb. 2.

The newes is that there hath beene a mutenie, or rather a massacre, of the Protestants, in some partes of Ireland.

<hr>

[a] The allusion is to the prosecution in the Star-chamber of the earl of Bedford, sir Robert Cotton, Selden, and others, which was made the pretence for locking up the Cottonian Library. Biographia Britannica, iv. 301, edit. Kippis.

Marriners are pressed at London, some say because there is a navy of the French feared, &c. Gulles. *Feb. 2.*

Greate talke of 32 (some say) articles of observation for the clergie, for lecturers and others, &c. *Feb.*

Three embassadors at London, France, Spaine, Venice.

The ships be set to sea for Newe England, February, and for a plantation neere Mexico also (*ut dicitur*). Newes of an heathen prince baptised at London. *New England.*

Some of the released parliament men sore fined. Hill. terme. *Parliament men.*

*Feb.*

### TO THE KING'S MOST EXCELLENT MAJESTIE [a]

The humble petition of the lord viscount Falkland, one of the lordes of his Majesties most hon. privy councell; most humbly shewing that I had a sonne, untill I lost him in your highnes displeasure, where I cannot seeke him, because I have no will to find him there. Men say that there is a wild young man, nowe prisoner in the Fleete for measuring his actions by his owne private sense; but now that for the same your Majesties hand hath appeered in the punishment, he bowes and humbles himselfe before and to it. Whether he be mine or not, I cannot discerne by any light but that of your royall clemency; for only in this [b] forgivenes must I owne him mine; forgivenes is the glory of the supreme powers, and this the operation,[c] that when it is extended in the greatest measure it converts the greatest offenders into the greatest lovers, and so makes purchase of the hearte, in [d] especiall priviledge peculier and due to soveraigne princes. If your Majestie will vouchsafe, out of your owne benignity, to become a second nature, and restore that unto me which the first gave and vainly[e] deprived me of, I shall keepe the reckoning of the full number of my sonnes with comforte, and render the tribute of my most humble thankfulnes; else my weak ould memory must forget one.　And pray.

*Carie viscount Falkland.*

*For a challenge of a duell.*

---

[a] Collated with a copy in Harl. MS. 3638, f. 140.

[b] "your," Harl. MS.　　　[c] "hath this operation," Ibid.

[d] "an," Ibid.　　　[e] "vanitie," Ibid.

Moonday the 8th of March, at Thetford assises, in the forenoon (I being present), the high constables being sworne (who then li open to such danger), complained, one of 8 pound drawne from him another of 4, the third of 30*s.* who was one James of Rockland [a] o Ellingham.[b] Presently after there was another voice, and a young man with ij of mr. sheriffe's men (sir Roger Townsend), brought in a purse-picker, a lusty young man, well apparelled, booted, and spurred. At his comming in he was asked, What countryman? he said, a Lincolnshire man. Where he dwelled; he said, at Roiston What his name was; he said, Musgrave. To other questions propounded by judge Hide, he answered, that he was going to sir John Hubberdes; that he had a letter thither; that his other busines he would keepe to himselfe; that he was an embroiderer; that he was not at Bury (but he lyed); that he laye at Barton milles, at the Bull, the night before; that he dranke only at the Bell in Thetford; that (here he paused) he had beene in the towne about halfe an houre; that he had no horse, but was a footeman. The young man said, that comming up the staires, at the dore to the north, he felte an hand in his pocket, and turning about, this man was by; and mr. sherif's men did chalenge him to have had his hand in his pocket, which both did affirme. My lord gave charge to mr. Hoberd (sir John was not then come) sir John's brother, to goe downe and take his examination, charging that they should looke that he dropped nothing, and searche him all over. He did confesse that he had about 28*s.*, but being serched (as I heard) he had 30*s.* and more found about him. James, before mentioned, that lost 30*s.*, found an halfe-crowne silver and 4*d. ob.*, also eight or ten farthings amongst this money, and some other pieces that were likely to be his, but would affirme no further upon his triall (as is reported), when there came a stranger, and affirmed that a yeere or two since the same

---

[a] There are several parishes of that name, with some distinctive affix, in Shropham hundred, Norfolk.

[b] Parish in the hundred of Shropham, co. Norfolk.

Musgrave or Stanley (so they say was his name), was taken at East
Dereham upon suspition and had before a justice, but escaped.
The jury found him guilty. The judge commended them. On
Wednesday he had judgment to die. His progresse was thus: Cutpurse pro-
Moonday he was taken and examined. Tuisday he was arraigned gresse.
and convicte. Wednesday had his judgment. Thursday he was
hanged. I tould diverse that I had noted him at Brandon ᵃ fayer,
and that Mr. Keene knewe him, who told me since that about two
yeeres past he had him and others to Sir William Spring, but he
escaped, and lay at Ixworth ᵇ on Friday; and at Thetford on Saturday he drewe a purse, and then went to the gaole and dranke with
the prisoners, where he escaped, for search was made for him upon
reporte that such an one came from Ixworth ᵇ that morning. Tuisday the 16th of March, Mr. Snelling, of Thetford, tould me that
this fellowe Stanley did shewe before his death the nickes upon a
staffe for every purse that he had taken, to the number of ninety-
three; also that he had revealed to the judge that there was a company of them at London, with a maister of them; that London was
limited out to them by theire numbers, that one might not meddle
in another's precincts; that twenty of them, five, five, five, and five,
attended on the Assises in four circuits; that his four fellowes were
fledde; that he had his dwelling in a street of London that he
named, &c.

March 22. Mr. Pratte tould me, that of late many Englishmen March 22.
went to masse at the queenes courte and the embassador's lodgings,
which caused a proclamation for restraint, upon paine of the execution of penall statutes; but when this was not sufficient, pursevants
were sent, who imprisoned many.ᶜ The queene made suite for
theire release, and had this answere from the King: " I permitte
you your religion with your Capuchins and others; I permitte

---

ᵃ County of Suffolk.                        ᵇ Near Bury St. Edmund's.
  ᶜ This proclamation does not appear in the Fœdera. It is alluded to in a news-letter,
Court and Times of Charles I. vol. ii. p. 67.

embassadors and theire retinue, but the rest my subjects I will have them live in the religion that I professe and my Father before me," &c.

He tould me also, that lately the plague being brought out of France into London, there died twenty in one weeke; but by God's mercy, care, and oversight, there died but four the next weeke; God continue his mercy towardes us.

He tould me further of 150 Hollanders' ships sent out to the West Indies, divided into three companies of fifty. One company met with 100 Spanish sent for garde, and fought long with them, yet overmastered, so that they many sunke themselves. The Spanyards, sore beaten, were met with soone by other fiftie, who then prevailed, and have sunke and taken most of those 100, and are gone to theire last fifty, who together have made some returne home, and the rest waite there for the silver fleete.

Sermon at the Assises.

Moonday, March 8. One Mr. Ramsey, whom Sir Roger Townsend, high sheriffe, had preferred to an impropriation in him appropriated (as is said), preached before the judges at Thetford, upon Isaiah i. 26,[a] as it seemed. I heard but the latter ende, which was wonderous pithy; full of all good wordes and all learning. He had many touches upon the corruptions of judges and councellors. A similitude he had of the head receiving all the nourishment, and causing the other members to faile and the whole man to die, which he applied to the commonwealth, where all is sucked upwards and the commons left without nourishment. Also of a fish that first putrifies at the heade, so some commonwealth. He touched upon the favouring of causes, and making all sound well on the favoured side and so on the contrary extenuating the greatest proofes on the side not favoured, &c.; he touched the Councell also for taking fees to be silent. He apologised (*ut dicitur*) before and after, saying

---

[a] " And I will restore thy judges as at the first, and thy counsellors as at the beginning; afterward thou shalt be called the city of righteousness, the faithful city."

that judges and all must learne at the lips of the priest.   Sale of
offices and simony he pithily set out, &c.

In Easter terme, writtes went out of the Exchequer to gentlemen
of 40 li. annuat., that were not at the King's coronation, to receive
knighthood.[a]

Plague at Cambridge.                                           Aprill.

Many noblemen died at Penbrooke, (Shrewsbury,) lord Wootton, Apr.
earl of Anglesey;[b] (some say lord Scroope).

At the Generall [Sessions] at Swafham, we received articles thus: Apr.

### Directions for the Ministers and Churchwardens of the severall parishes of the archdeaconry of Norfolk.

1. His Majestie's declaration, published anno domini 1628, before Articles.
the articles of religion for setling all questions in difference, must be
strictly observed.

2. Speciall care must be had concerning lecturers in every parish,
for whom these directions ensuing are to be observed.

[1.[c] In all parishes, the afternoon sermons must be turned into
catechising by question and answer, where and whensover there is
no great cause apparent to breake this ancient and profitable order.

[2. Every lecturer shall read divine service according to the
liturgie printed by authority, in his surplice and hood, before the
lecture.

[3. Where any lecture is set up in a market towne, the same
shall be read by a company of grave and orthodox divines neere
adjoyning in the same diocesse, and they are to preach in gownes
and not in cloakes, as many use to doe].

If a corporation doe mainteine a single lecturer, he must not be

---

a See Rushworth, pt. ii. vol. i. p. 70.

b George Talbot, earl of Shrewsbury, and Thomas lord Wotton, but not the earl of
Anglesey.   There was no lord Scrope at this date.   The title became extinct in 1627.

c Rushworth, part ii. vol. i. p. 30, gives the five following directions, but not the
remainder of the document.

suffered to preach till he professe his willingnes to take upon him a
living with cure of soules within that incorporation; and he must
actually take such benefice or cure so soone as it shall be fairely
procured for him.

3. The minister and churchwardens in every parish, or one of
them, are at these Generals and at every General hereafter to certifie in theire verdicts the christian names and surnames of every
lecturer in theire parish, and the place where he preacheth, together
with his quality and degree.

4. They are in like manner to certifie the names of such men as
being not qualified by lawe doe keepe chaplens in theire houses.

5. They are further to certifie the names of all such as absent
themselves from or are negligent in comming to divine service, as
well prayers as catechisings and sermons.

6. The minister and churchwardens of every parish successively
are to keepe a severall copie of these instructions by them, whereby
they may be the better informed of theire duty; and the said
copies are to be shewed at every Generall, when they shall present
all such persons as have disobeyed these instructions; that, according to his Majesties pleasure, such as doe conforme may be encouraged, and such as are refractory may be punished.

These articles, thus received in one halfe sheete, printed we
knowe not where, seeme to come from the King, in what sorte we
knowe not; only this is knowne, that they want the ordinary rati-
fication; " By the King."

Aprill.  The plague at Cambridge, where many houses be infected; the
commencement put of untill October; the colledges broken up;
many townesmen departed.

May.  It encreaseth also at London; and three houses shut up in
Norwich.

Prince borne.  May the 30th, as it is said, was our young prince borne, for
which there were signes of greate joy on Tuisday, June 1, at Thetford.  God give us all joy of him !  He was borne betweene the two

eclipses, one of the moone, May 16, and the other of the sunne, May 31, at six or seven at night. (*Fertur*) borne May 30, at two in the morning.

June 7. At Bury I heard glances of jelousie.

The same day I had a note given me of Dr. Layton's trouble for writing a booke.[a]   *A mistake, for it was against the bishops.*[b]

The same day it was tould me that on Sunday, May 30, the Londoners shewed theire joy for the prince; and then at nine the King received the sacrament at Paule's, and came to the sermon, which (as I heard before) a Suffolke man made, upon Judges xiv. 18: "If ye had not plowed, &c. ye had not expounded my riddle;" then, after the sermon, he gave the City thankes for theire rejoicings.

*All might arise from some fellowes disallowing of the king and queen's match, some Puritan.*

*And offered to the altar 100 pieces.*

The same, June 7, I received at Bury these verses:

Dum Rex Paulinas accessit gratus ad aras,
    Emicuit medio lucida stella die :
Dic, divina mihi tractans enigmata, præco
    Hæc nobis oriens quid sibi stella velit,
Magnus in occiduo princeps modo nascitur orbe,
    Crasque sub ecclipsyn regna orientis erant.

Some litle while since, the company went to Newe England under Mr. Wintrop.   Mr. Cotton, of Boston in Lincolnshire, went to theire departure about Gravesend, and preached to them, as we heare, out of 2 Samuel, vii. 10.   It is said, that he is prohibited for preaching any more in England then untill June 24 next now

*June 7.*

<hr/>

[a] Alexander Leighton, a Scotchman, first a physician, then a divine. He wrote two works : " The Looking Glass of the Holy War," and " Zion's Plea against Prelacy," in both of which the bishops are roughly handled, and for which he was severely punished. See pp. 54, 55, *infra;* and Rushworth, vol. i. pt. ii. pp. 55-58. The particulars of his seizure are given in the Court and Times of Charles I. vol. i. pt. ii. p. 61; and of his punishment, pp. 80-85.

[b] Inserted afterwards.

comming. I sawe a booke at Bury at a bookeseller's, conteining a
declaration of theire intent who be gone to Newe England, set out
by themselves, and purposed for satisfaction to the King and state
(as I conceive), because of some scandalous misconceivings that
runne abroade.

1572, the like there.

Some say a starre was seene at noone by diverse in Paul's church-
yard. They say that one Perkins, a gentleman, affirmes a precon-
tract of the queene, and thereupon called the prince a .[b] He
is like to be hanged, drawne, and quartered.

Doctor Layton.

Doctor Layton, a Scot, hath lost his eares (*ut dicitur*).[c]

Prince Charles baptised.

The 27th of June the prince was baptised by the name of
Charles; the king of France was godfather and the Palsgrave, the
queen mother of France godmother. The young duke of Lennox
represented the king of France, marquess Hambleton earl of Cambridge the Palsgrave, the countesse of Penbroke the queene
mother.[d] The nurse had 1000 *li.* The mayor of London sent a
silver fonte, wherein he was baptised. A generall pardon and
release of many prsioners. Thus is the reporte.

> When private men get sonnes, they gette a spoone,[e]
> Without eclipse or any starre at noone;
> When kings get sonnes, they get withall supplies,
> And succours farre beyond five subsidies.[f]

---

[a] Query, "New England's Trials, declaring the successe of twenty-six ships employed thither within these six yeares, with the benefit of that country by sea and land, and how to build three score sayle of good ships to make a little navie royall," by Capt. John Smith, 4to. Lond. 1620.

[b] Blank in MS.

[c] See Rushworth, pt. ii. vol. i. p. 58.

[d] This is a mistake, the queen mother was represented by the duchess of Richnond.

[e] Referring to the practice of sponsors giving spoons. See Shakespeare's Henry VIII. act v. scene ii.

[f] "All subsidies" in Gilchrist's Collection of Corbet's Poems, 12mo. Lond. 1807, p. 148.

Welcome, God's loane, greate tribute of the state,        Knight-mony.
Thou mony new come in,[a] rich fleete of plate;
Welcome, blest babe,[b] whom God thy father sent
To make him rich without a parliament.

Finis qd. RICH. OXON.

Those verses, pp. 68, 69,[c] doe not seeme to be his that made these. Rich. Oxon. may be subscribed by some other, and it may be by such an one as is in the former termed Puritan.

The plague was sore at Cambridge this summer, so that there was no Sturbridge fayer; and in the beginning of this October (the midsommer commencement having fayled and the fayer), for the benefit of university officers, there was a commencement wherein many went out, doctors, bachelers of divinity, &c. at a cheape rate; the plague being not ceased there yet. And at London it encreaseth (as is said) to eighty in a weeke. The terme that was put of untill November 1, some thinke will be stayed longer. *(Plague at Cambridge and London.)*

About Michaelmas the king's Whelpe, that (as it seemeth) Lynne men had obteined this summer to garde theire fleete, being returning, tooke a Dunkerke by the way, betweene Yermouth and Lowistofte, in the boarding of which, by some mischance, some gunpowder in it was so fired by a candle or the like, that the ship was blowne in pieces, so that the maine was sunke, many were hurte, some drowned, and some fewe escaped sound. The Dunkerke was taken by other ships neere. *(The king's whelpe.)*

Doctor Layton, of whom pp. 78, 79,[d] was this Michaelmas terme punished with whipping, the losse of one eare, and the slitting of one nostrill; the like punishment being reserved (*ut dicitur*) untill the next terme. It is said, that he denied the penning of the booke; and perhaps, had he not fledde, he had not thus beene punished. The tale goeth, that a tayler of London came into his prison, in whose cloake he escaped, and went forty miles from Lon- *(Doctor Layton.)*

[a] "Newly coined," Sloane MS.      [b] "Thrice happy," Ibid.
[c] See pp. 42, 43, *supra*.      [d] See pp. 53, 54, *supra*.

don; whereat the King said thus: " He hath saved me the labour of banishing him;" but Dr. Laud, bishop of London, not so satisfyed, gate him discovered, and so returning, he was thus censured. His escape made him the rather to be judged guilty.

**Knight mony.** The mony for not appeering to be knighted was lately gathered up.

**Peace with Spaine.** December 5. A peace with Spaine proclaimed, with much ringing and many bonefiers.[a] It is said the Spanish embassador,[b] comming to the King to congratulate, fell all along, and shedde abundance of teares, not feined perhaps, but out of griefe of the Spanish dishonour in seeking this peace.

**October. Commencement.** A commencement of many doctors, thirty-two some say; and twenty-six of them of the plague.[c] The plague had pulled the **No Sturbridge fayer. See p.80.[d]** university and towne of Cambridge. No Sturbridge fayer. **King of Sweden.** The king of Sweden is to have soldiers out of England and Scotland. He shall mainteine the Germane warre. The Spanyard must restore what he hath of the Palatinate.

**Dearth.** Wheate 28s. the combe; rie 24s. and 26s.; barly 18s. and 20s.

**King and Queene. See p. 46.[e]** The King and Queene at Newmarket about January 14.

January 19, 1630. It was my hap to be at Reiningham in Norfolk, within j mile of Hales, where I learned this to perfecte the story, page 46. One William Alexander, whose father lived at Stokesby in Fleg,[f] and his brother at Loddon neere Hales,[g] was in league with a maide in Stokesby (by him gotten with child), and with the daughter of one      [h] Whitlo of Hales, both at once. This Whitloe's daughter he was to carry to Norwich, on a Saturday, there to marry her (whether this following matter stayed the marriage that day or not, I remember not what was tould me), and the day before, at Stokesby, he so dealte with the other at Stokesby, that he pro-

---

[a] Fœdera, vol. viii. pt. iii. p. 136.      [b] Don Carlos de Colonna.
[c] So in the MS. The death of many doctors seems to be meant.
[d] See p. 55, *supra*.      [e] See p. 24, *supra*.      [f] East Flegg, co. Norfolk.
[g] Parish in the hundred of Clavering, co. Norfolk.      [h] Blank in MS.

cured her to steale out, and to waite for him at a certaine place, untill night, when he came to her, to carrie her on horsebacke to Norwich, there to marrie her.  She being behind him, complained that he went out of his way, which he did indeede, and carried her over Reedham ᵃ Fery in the night (where a fisherman discovered them), and so rode to Hales.  At Hales, neere Whitloe's house, he caused the wench to alight and goe over an hedge, purposing to followe with his horse, but could not untill she came backe, and drave him over; after which he ledde her to a place in the close, where was (unknowne to her) a deepe well that was covered with some blockes, and, over them, brambles or the like.  There they continued a while, and in the end she was put into the well about the beginning of daylight.  He went streight away to the house, and called, telling them there that it was daylight.  The wench being missed at Stokesby, enquiry was soone made at Whitloe's for this fellowe, who, perceiving the men, wished Whitloe's wife (or widowe rather perhaps) to tell them he was not there, but she refused, and made him to shewe his face unto them.  They asked for the wench, but he would confesse nothing; whereupon they gate a justice's warrant, and tooke him the next day morning, as he was going to his brother at Loddon.  The justice made a mittimus, yet he continued a while under the constable's handes, and at length his brother and another did baile him; but his brother soone, upon conference with him, suspected something, and gate released: so he was sent to prison. He had said to some-bodie, that where ever she was they could not come at her.  Many thoughts were working upon this matter, and, although the wench saith that on Tuisday after (for so it was found to agree with the time, when one was chopping and sizing of billet neere the well,) she heard the noise of chopping, yet then she was not knowen to be there, for she feared least he or some other should have throwne downe something upon her.  But on Wednesday a

The maide in the well.

ᵃ Parish in Walsham hundred, co. Norfolk.

maide from Whitloe's house going to make hay espyed the tracke
of his horse over the hedge, which she followed even to the well;
where stooping downe, she hearde the wench. Hereupon transported,
she runneth away, and meeting some, she cried still, " The well, the
well, the well, the well !" with which wordes she went to the smithes
shop, and the smith and another observing her, she beckened and
ran to the well, where about the midday, by helpe of a ladder and
ropes, she came forthe.  She had no hurte, nor scarce any shewe of
any, notwithstanding there were blockes at the bottom of the well,
which strange accident they impute to her clothes, which with
gathering of wind might breake the falle.  She saith she dranke her
owne water, and that there were mise and other filthy vermin in the
bottome.  She being often examined, held one tale still; viz. that
she knoweth not how she came into the well, and was so silent in
her evidence against him, not saying that he tooke any thing from
her, that the judge sawe her intent, and gave her a caveat to feare
him afterward, yet she is married to him, and liveth now with him.
Whitloe's company used her kindly, and her child miscarried not,
but lived.

At that place, I learned that one Playfer of Stocton ᵃ left a sonne
and two daughters, to whom he gave and entayled his land, and
after them to his wife, who married and had children by a second
husband.  The sonne growne up was enticed to goe to London,
with a lewd fellowe, one        Fortune, with whom and one Worlich (if not Laud also), he was last seene at Holton Hill by Hals-
worth.ᵇ  The elder sister was missed, and the younger was drowned
in taking up a little water at a pit to washe some pot.  This by the
countries surmise may appertaine to the story of 3 carkases found in
a pond at Halesworth, which caused Laud to be hanged, Worlich
condemned, and Mr. Norton to be troubled.  See Mr. Couper's
booke too, soone published, and my notes elsewhere.

3 carkases in
the ponde.

ᵃ A parish in Clavering hundred, co. Norfolk.
ᵇ Holton is 1¼ miles from Halesworth, hundred of Blything, co. Suffolk.

March 6.   The newes is that the king of Sweden hath declared King of Sweden.
his reasons why he taketh up armes against the emperor.   1. The
emperor's forces, in proper colours, bare armes against him in Poland.
2. An ancient firme league there was and is betweene him and the
duke of Pomeran, whom the emperor enfesteth.   3. An ancient
league also betweene Sweden and the States of Germany, wherefore Sweden.
he will not lay downe his armes untill Germany be *in statu quo
prius*.   The newes is also that the emperor hath called a diet, and
demanded 3 things.   1. Monyes to oppose the king of Sweden.
2. The confirmation of the Palatinate Electorship upon Bavaria.
3. That his sonne be made king of Romans.   All three are denied,
and the princes resolved never to chuse emperor of the house of
Austria againe.

Newes that the king and the queene mother be at variance; that France.
the queene is driven into a city, and there besieged, upon some March 6.
treason against the king's person.

Newes that the Spanish embassador is departed discontente, England.
because of 4,000 Scottes that be gone to aide the Sweden king.

The emperor hath called a diet, and requested three things:    Newes.
1. Supplies of mony for to withstand Swethland's king.    March 3.
2. The confirmation of the Electorship of the Palatinate upon
Bavaria.
3. The enstalling of his owne sonne king of Romans.

All three be denied, and, as it is said, a vowe is made not to have
any emperor more of the house of Austria.

The king of Sweden doth prevaile against the emperor.   The King of Sweden.
Archduches hath demolished her fortes in Cleveland, and that
corner.

The king of Spaine is dead, as the newes comes Apr. 25.    King of Spaine
Aprill.   The newes was that the Hollanders had againe met with dead.   False.
Spaine's silver fleete, and taken greate treasure from him.

The newes was also that there is greate store of silver ingots or Silver minted.
bullion now at our minte; from Spaine some say.

Lord Awdley
beheaded.

A beast dead.

The lord Awdley (earl of Castelhaven in Ireland as some say,
for causing his daughters to be ravished before his face; as som
say, for Sodom: besides, was put to death about May 14, at th
Tower.  Some say he was put to death for procuring the ravish
ment of his wife, he holding her forcibly in the time, and also fo
Sodom: with a page.  The agents in the rape shall die also.  The
say he was arraigned by the name of Mervin lord Awdley.  H
denied these crimes, but confessed himselfe worthy of death.  H
was first (he said) a Protestant, and then became Papist, in whicl
profession he sawe so much loosenes that he grewe dissolute, anc
never after thrived in soule, body, credit, or estate.  Thus gentle
men reporte.[a]

Hollanders get
more treasure.

It was reported, soone after the peace with Spain, 1630, page
81, that diverse of our ships arriving in Spain were there stayed
because the silver fleete was then coming home; and since it i
reported that the Hollanders have met with that fleete, and gotter
the chiefe treasure.

May.

Gilly cut her
owne throate at
Bury.

About the middest of May, on a Wednesday night, the daughter
of one Gilly deceased (living in the widowe Tillot's house), a maide
thought to be very religious, and having had 7 or 8 sc.[b] pound
in her owne hand, did rise out of her bed, as is said, and, going into
a wood-chamber, cutte her owne throate, lefte the knife in the
wound, fell grobling (her armes being foulded) at the head of
payre of staires, and bled abundantly; being thereby found the next
morning.  Diverse lately have hanged themselves at Linne,[c] Bran
don,[c] Elmswell,[d] Finborough.[d]

Plague.
May.

The plague at Wimondham [e] and diverse townes thereabout, very
sore.  They say it is yet in Lincolneshire.

[a] See Rushworth, pt. ii. vol. i. pp. 93-103.
[b] Score.
[c] In Norfolk.
[d] In Suffolk.
[e] In the hundred of Forehoe, co. Norfolk.

June 13.  Anthony Rous, my father, of All Saints in Weeting,[a] parson, from June 1600, died.[b]

That day at night, Sir Martin Stutvill, of Dalham,[c] comming from the Sessions at Bury, with Sir George le Hunt, went into the Angell, and there being mery in a chayer, either readie to take tobacco, or having newly done it, (ut fertur) leaned backward with his head, and died immediatlie. Sir Martin Stutvill dieth sodainly.

July 18, were executed at Bury 13; whereof iij., a boy of 16 and ij. women, were executed for burning of Walderswicke,[d] in Suffolk.  The boy, upon his death, affirmed that his sister councelled, and the other woman (who was begotten with child by Nathan Browning of Dennington,[e] before marriage,) gave him fire.  They both affirmed themselves cleere.  The sister confessed there, before Mr. Ward, her falte in standing excommunicate.  The boy, they say, was borne at Wimondham,[f] in the yeere of the fire there.  Forty houses were burned, June 10, or thereabout, and 8 at a second time, July 3, being Sunday.  After this it was discovered. July. Walderswike burnte.

About this time were gone and going diverse voluntaries, gathered up by the drumme, to goe with marques Hamilton to the helpe of the king of Swedeland, in the German warres. Marques Hamilton gathereth voluntaries.

Together with reporte of the king of Sweden's besieging of Magdenburg, which Tilly had taken this summer and burnt, killing all without mercy,[g] it was said, upon Sir Thomas Jermin's worde that our agent in Poland had written thus to our King.  The queen of September. Papists denie this, but I believe it is the truth in the generall.

[a] A parish in the hundred of Grimshoe, co. Norfolk.

[b] In the list of the clergy of Weeting, occurs the following : " 1600, June 25, Anthony Rouse.  Agnes Wright and Thomas Wright, by grant of the presentation from Sir Robert Wyngfield, Knight, &c.  He was buried 13th June, 1631.  In his answer to King James's Queries in 1603, he says there were 104 communicants here."  Bloomfield's Norfolk, 8vo. edit. vol. ii. p. 170.

[c] A parish in the hundred of Risbridge, co. Suffolk.

[d] Or Walberswick, hundred of Blything.

[e] Near Framlingham, co. Suffolk.

[f] Hundred of Forehoe, co. Norfolk—spelled Wymondham, or Windham.

[g] See Rushworth, pt. ii. vol. i. p. 135.

Poland and her Jesuites and Priests made a greate triumph for
Tillie's taking of Magdenburg, erecting Calvin's and Luther's
statues in ij. postes, which they burned with an hellish greate fire;
but in returning, most of the Priests and Jesuites were killed by fier
from heaven, and the queene stroken madde, and as is thought
thereupon soone deade.[a] Mr. Jenkenson.[b]

*Dead she is. The Polish embassador at London, caused the courte to mourne.*[c]

*Windham plague.*

The plague at Wimondham, they say, is neere ceased nowe, this
Sept. 8, and a market kept somewhere since.

*Sermons against the judges.*

Summer assises at Bury had one Mr. Scot, of Ipswich, that
preached before the judges, who made a sore sermon in discovery of
corruptions of judges and others. At Norwich Mr. Greene was
more plaine, insomuch that Judge Harvy, in his charge, brake
out thus—" It seemes by the sermon that we are corrupt, but know
that we can use conscience in our places, as well as the best clergie
man of all." Judge Hide died this harvest. Judge Richardson, in

*Sir N. Hide dies, &c.*

the West, had a prisoner that cast a stone at him, and smote his hat
of, as is reported. And one Sir [d] Pie, a judge in the marches of
Wales, was by a Welche man that thought himselfe wronged thrust
in, and wounded with his sworde.

*A victory at Bergen.*

The Hollanders had a greate victory at Bergen-ap-Zoom. The
enemie had prepared in secret boates, shipping, and other things for
surprisall of it (or for landing and intrenching, so as in time to have
wunne it). They landed, and the reporte of theire ordinance brought
the Prince of Orange, who was some miles of, with his companies
thether, with some 8,000 men, who routed them, ere they could be
entrenched, and killed 7 or 8,000, and tooke many prisoners, and
much spoile.

*Jesuites converted in Ireland.*

The reporte is that 4 Jesuites in Ireland do preach the Gospell,
and doe much good.

<hr/>

[a] The report of her sudden death, on the very day in which a procession celebrating the
victories of the Romish party took place, was correct: and also that the thunder and
lightning were very violent on that day. See Court and Times of Charles I. vol. ii. p. 166.

[b] Probably the name of the person who gave this information.

[c] Added later.      [d] Blank in MS.

The Fennes be in draining, and a newe river is cut and casting up at Litleporte, ª or thereabout. New river.

The reporte is that Saxonie now joyneth with the king of Sweden, who prevaileth against Tilly. Saxonie joyneth.

October 14, newes from Cambridge that there was a greate fight betweene the king of Sweden with the duke of Saxony, and Tilly on the other side. Tilly was taken, and is deade;ᵇ his whole army dispersed, &c. The king carried the duke among the slaine, and asked him how he liked of it. The duke said it was a sad spectacle. "Well," said the king, "all this you are the cause of; for, if you had not stood neuter at the first, this had beene prevented." Tilly bewailed his unfortunatenes, since he cruelly massacred them of Magdenburgh, which he did at the emperor's especiall command. Tilly overc.

Sir Nicholas Hide, Lorde Chiefe Justice of England, or of the King's Bench, died immediatly after his departing from summer assises at Norwich. Some say he was poysened by a petition there; others that he gate the plague so, and died thereof. Sir Nicholas Hide.

Sir Thomas Richardson in his place, at the beg.ᶜ of Michael-mas terme, and Sir Robert Heath, the King's Atturny, is Lord Chief Justice of the Common Pleas. Sir Thomas Richardson.

Cambridge is wonderously reformed since the plague there; schol-lers frequent not the streetes and tavernes, as before; but doe worse.ᵈ Cambridge reformed.

The king of Sweden hath given the emperor a greate overthrowe, all Tillie's companies slaine and dispersed. King of Sweden.

A young princes borne here, Nov. 3, at night.ᵉ Princesse born November.
The duke of Orleans arrived here in England.

A booke came to my handes, printed 1631, by R. Y., for Jo. Partridge, called "God's power and providence in preserving 8 Englishmen, left by mischance in Greenland, 1630, nine monthes 8 men left at Greenland.

ª In the Isle of Ely.

ᵇ Incorrect. Tilly was shot near Ingoldstadt, 30th April, 1632.

ᶜ Beginning.

ᵈ Added afterwards.          ᵉ Mary, afterwards princess of Orange.

and twelve days, reported by Edward Pelham, one of y<sup>e</sup> 8."<sup>a</sup> William Fakeley, gunner; Edward Pelham, gunner's mate; John Wise, and Robert Goodfellow, seamen; Thomas Ayers, whale-cutter; Henry Bette, cooper; John Dawes, and Richard Kellet, landmen.  The booke conteyneth a mappe of Greenland, lying from 77 N.L. to 80; with it a whale described (which is ordinarily 60 foote long); his fashion somewhat like a gogeon.  Also the manner of taking, killing, cutting; boiling of him; a description of a sea-morce, as big as an oxe, &c.  The principall things be these which he reporteth.  The countrie is mountainous, full of ice and snowe; the plaines most parte bare.  There growes no tree nor herbe, but scurvy grasse and sorrell.  The sea affordes whales, sea-horses, seales, and other small fish.  They went in the Salutation of London, May 1, 1630, and arrived in Greenland June 11.  There were three ships, under the command of Captain William Goodler, who sent a command to the Salutation beforesaid to come to him to an harbour called Bell Sownd; upon which these men, being on land killing of deere, and by mists and other accidents hindered, were lefte at Greenland, from about August 20 untill 25th of May, without company and comfort; for these climates are not inhabited. Our merchants could never hire any to winter there.  They wintered at Bell Sownd, in an house of timber and dealeborde, 80 foote long, builded by Dutchmen.  In this they builded a lesser, with deale, brickes, lime, &c., brought thither; and especially filling between inner dealebords and outward with sand, to keepe out the could; and had no windowes, but opened a tile or two aloft; 4 cabins they builded within, and billetted by 2 and 2, lodging in deere's skinnes dryed.  There fuell was ould shallops unserviceable, lefte there from yeere to yeere; empty caskes, plankes, and coolers, what might not hinder the next yeere's voyage.  A piece of sheetelead

<sup>a</sup> It was printed separately, 4to. London, 1631, and is reprinted in Churchill's Voyages, vol. ii.

being found upon one of the coolers, they made of it lampes, to
burne some naughty refuse oyle, there lefte in them, for theire lights, Rope yarne.
in which they put for the wike twists of ould ropes.    They killed
venison, some sea-horse, and beares, of whose flesh and the friclers
or granes of the whales they did eate, and so preserved themselves.
From October 14 to February 9, they sawe no sunne, but the moone
alwaies.   (They found some spring water, under a thicke ice, and
for the rest they dranke snowe water, melted by hote irons.)   Yet
by the last of January, he saith that the dayes were seven or eight
houres long.    That is, dayes yet without sunne, for he said before
from the December 1 to the 20 there was no light, but sometimes
a small glare of white towards the south.    In the spring they gate
some fowles, and one of theire mastive dogs went forth and never
returned.    About May 28, Hull men came, who haled them with
" hey;" they returned " ho;" and so were these comforted, the other
amazed.    May 28, London fleete came, wherein these 8 returned
August 20, and came all safe and whole to London.    All they say
of the cold is that, touching of iron, theire hands hung too, as to
bird-lime; and looking out, they were sore nipped, and proved so
as if they had beene beaten.

It is nowe talked that the king of Sweden is in the Palatinate; November.
some say at Prague, and that the Palsgrave shall goe up in the King of
spring, with 24,000 ; that the Duke of Saxony is in Silesia, and Sweden.
Marques Hamilton.    That the king of Sweden and his aide is If Protestants
80,000; that the duke of Loraine will helpe the emperor (but this pursue not this
may be a giere); Grebner would be observed in many particulars.[a] sotted.

---

[a] Paulus Grebnerus, who came over to England in 1582, presented queen Elizabeth
with a MS. in Latin, containing predictions of the future history of Europe, which excited
a good deal of attention, on account of the verification of many of his predictions, more
particularly those relating to Gustavus Adolphus.    The MS. was deposited in Trinity
College, Cambridge.    See a memorandum at the end of Harl. MS. 6882, which is tran-
scribed from a loose sheet, printed May 1649, of which a copy is among the King's
Pamphlets, British Museum, in folio.    There is a brief extract from Grebner's prophecy

CAMD. SOC.                         K

Imbellis Rodolphus.ᵃ Deus excitat Electorem Sax. Decretum re
gium, &c. In hoc concuss. et classico tumultu, &c. Omnes simu
obmutescetis denudatim. Sed nobilis heros Suecicus. Locuples
&c. Inuicte Philippe,ᵇ (an ironie sure,) and in other things.

*November 29.*
*Warres with Spain.*

The newes came that our truce with Spaine was out; that ou
English were forbidden traffique with Spaine; it may be so intended
but it is not so yet. Newes also by Mr. Tayler, that a Jesuite at
Strasborough, after the Swethish victory, made his prayer to thi

*A Jesuites prayer against heretiks.*
*All heretiks were touched.*

effecte: " Lords and ladies, let us pray to God and to the blessed
Virgin, to cause her Sonne to preserve us in the Catholike religion
to defend us against the devill of Sweden, and all his helpes, the
conjurers and witches of Lapland, by whose enchantments thes
Swedish devills flie about among us; from the bloud hounds the
States, and all theire councels; from the adders of England and al
theire frends; from the beggerly Lutheran princes, that they get no
head against us," &c. (This was the summe; Mr. Taylor hath a
copie.) For all the devils conspire this 1631.

*November.*

About the beginning of this month was the murther at Harelston.
Bucke, clerke of Rednall,ᵈ in the evening being upon the high way
in a footepath with a maide that he was welwiller to, was assaulted

*Murther at Rednall and Harleston.*

by            Warren (that was in beere) who urged upon the maide
to ride behinde him, &c. The issue was, that Bucke with hi
cooke's knife cut the throate of Warren's horse, and killed Warren
himselfe. November 15, this was tould me then at Henham,ᵉ or
rather the 16.

*November.*

15. I was at Halesw.ᶠ A youth at Lackford ᵍ by playing about

in Harl. MS. 4931, f. 13, in which the king of Sweden's successor, and the Popish queen
of king Charles are named.

ᵃ Rodolph II., emperor of Austria.          ᵇ Philip II. of Spain.
ᶜ Hundred of Stow, co. Suffolk.
ᵈ Redenhall, a parish one mile and a half from Harleston.
ᵉ The seat of the Rous family, in Wangford parish, Suffolk.
ᶠ Halesworth, a market town, hundred of Blything, co. Suffolk.
ᵍ Hundred of Thingoe, co. Suffolk.

a bedde of strawe that thatchers had made, fell so upon the thatcher's knife that it ranne into his body above an hand length, and killed him presently.    Mr. Francis Croftes tould this as done neere him at Lackford, as I conceived.

Certaine newes that Prague is taken and Bohemia revolted from the emperor.    That the pope sent a messenger to the king of Sweden, with congratulation for the victory he had against the emperor, is a thing not unlike.

December 3.
Prague taken.

December the 12th, at night as is thought, some West-country packman that had sold all in Norfolk, returned by Thetford, and went towards Barton milles[a] late; but the next morning three horses with pack saddles and two packes were found short of Elden a mile. These horses and packes are seised by the lord of Elden.    Some thinke a man is murthered and robbed; some thinke that it was a servant that is ridden away on the fourth horse with the mony. The packes were fish, either bought or trucked at Norwich or Yermouth.

Elden busines about three packhorses.

It was a servant that carried away what mony he had taken up, &c.

There came forth a booke called " The Swedish Intelligencer," which did set forthe the proceedings of the king of Sweden since his landing in Germany untill Michaelmas last.    By the way he speaketh of a generall desire of peace in Germany; but the way not found but by the union of Protestants.    Saxony and others at last meeting at Leipsich, and resolving to stand against the emperor for better union, decreed that both Calvinistes and Lutherans should be called Evangelici.    The king at first relieved some islands and Hans townes, upon the coastes of the Baltique sea, and at last comming up, joyned with the duke of Saxony, &c.; and gave Tilly that utter overthrowe in a pitchde field in the heath, God's-aker, neere Lipsich (for which God alwaies be praised!) the 7th of September.[b]    He tooke eighty towns in six or eight weekes, and since hath done, as we heare, what he listed in Bohemia and the Palatinate (whither

December.
The first parte of the Swedish Intelligencer.

[a] In the hundred of Lackford, co. Suffolk.
[b] See Rushworth, pt. ii. vol. i. pp. 107-110.

the Palsgrave is returned about February 6) keeping his Christmas in Mentz.

The said first parte, &c. produceth a piece of P. G. whom he stileth "the famous Paulus Grebnerus, whose booke lyeth in Trinity Colledge."[a]

It is since reported, that a fewe yeeres since, Sir Thomas Rolfe,[b] sent embassador to Moscow and Russia, dealt with the king of Sweden by the way, and told him the necessity of his engaging himselfe in this warre in regarde of his future safety, which he apprehended, yet excused himselfe by the greatnes of the warre, the neede of credite, countenance, meanes, and helpes to go thorough with it, and therefore he being of small reputation, &c. he durst not; but Sir Thomas promising assistants if he would begin, then he called a councell, who resolved of the said necessity for securing his kingdomes in future times; and so he prepared and undertooke, &c. Now lately, remembring the successe and his honor, he in a letter to Sir Thomas Rolfe, acknowledgeth with thankes the [c] he, next under God, was meanes of all this; and for a remembrance sends him 2400 *li.* in copper.

Li. in weight.

Lord chiefe justice.

Sir Thomas Richardson was removed from the Common pleas (against his mind for gaine) to the King's Bench, and Sir Robert Heath made lord chief justice of the Common pleas, who comes this circuite in Norfolk, &c. This was done princip. Term. Michaelmas.

Thirston.

Mr. Catlin's sermon.

Upon Shrovemoonday, February 13, Mr. Catlin, preaching at Bury, gave out before his sermon that it was good the ministers of the combination wold meete to consulte of the making of the combination, that those ministers that wold doe good might be put

---

[a] See note [a], p. 65, *supra.*

[b] This should be Sir T. Roe, who was ambassador to Turkey, and afterwards to Sweden, and was a warm friend of the Queen of Bohemia. The letter and present are mentioned in The Court and Times of Charles I. vol. ii. p. 143.

[c] that.

in seasonably for it.  I learned since that a newe-come minister Mr. Peed's Register hath swayed all.
was put in first in the combination, to beginne on Plough Moonday,
but as it seemed would not goe before the graver preachers, and
therefore lefte the day unprovided; but Mr. Catlin, by entreaty,
preached at that time, *ex improviso,* and after wold have beene freed In effecte so much.
of this his owne time, but could not (thus he said before the ser-
mon), and in his sermon said thus much obiter, which I heard:
"We are blamed for our churches, but it is certaine that these
courtes extracte more from us then will repayer our churches,
adorne them, and keepe them so."

On Tuisday the next day, being February 14, Shrove Tuisday, Mr. Garie's sermon.
Mr. Garie, of Becham,[a] preached at Methwold,[b] where I heard
him.  He preached in his cloake, read prayers so, without a sur- To use the surplis and a gowne are enjoyned in the combination upon the pulpit there.
plis (as I remember).  In reading whereof, he stayed for Mr. Pecke
and some others, to mutter eche other verse of the Psalmes; and
omitting a first lesson, he read a second lesson, wherein he mouthed
it Je—sus, with a lowe congie; and in his sermon upon Matthew, iii. 10,[c] among those whom he made liable to God's fearfull
judgment, against whom the axe is threatned, he named adulterers,
oppressors, atheists, those that bowed not at the name of Jesus,
and (I thinke also) those that were covered at divine service,
with others; in rehearsing of those not bowing, he produced
Philip. ii. 10,[d] how well convening let it be scanned; but, *O tem-
pora, qui pastores?*

The Palsgrave most joyfullie received, with great acclamations, February. Palsgrave.
in his Palatinate: "God save the King of Bohemia!"  Count Jo. of
Nassau defeated by the king of Sweden, as he went up against the
Palsgrave, &c.

[a] Beckham, hundred of Erpingham, co. Norfolk.

[b] Hundred of Grimeshoe, co. Norfolk.

[c] "And now also the axe is laid unto the root of the trees; therefore every tree which bringeth not forth good fruit is hewn down and cast into the fire."

[d] "That at the name of Jesus every knee should bow, of things in heaven, and things in earth, and things under the earth."

April 1, being Easter day, Doctor Buttes,[a] vice-chancellor of Cambridge, and maister of Bennet Colledge, did hang himselfe. The King and Queene were at Cambridge but a while before; something gave occasion.

The second parte of the Swedish Intelligencer is extant, declaring the actes of the Swedish king, the last summer 1632, ending before the last battell at Leipsich, about October, when it is said he was slaine.

About that very time, died the Palsgrave in his owne country.

Mr. Shervile [b] of Lincolne's Inne, recorder of Salisbury, was in Michaelmas terme censured in the Starre Chamber, for pulling downe a worshipped picture of God the Father, which was in a windowe of that church of Salisbury. If he had set a glasier to doe it, he had not beene questioned. Mr. Prin of the same house sent to the Tower about his booke Histriomastix.[c] Much to doe about ceremonies, high altar and copes, &c. at Paules. A cruell robbing murtherer hanged, at the way side beyond Ware, March 19, in chaines.

Diverse Irishmen so hanged at that time in Kent, for a cruell robbery and murther of many in one house.

London bridge burnte, February 11.

1633, April, I received these verses.

---

[a] Henry Butts, D.D. elected master of Corpus Christi or Benet college 1626. His suicide created a great sensation. In a letter to the fellows of Corpus Christi college, dated the 2d of April, the King says, "You can hardly conceive how we are affected with the untimely and precipitated death of Dr. Butts, our vice-chancellor and master of that our colledge in our university of Cambridge, wherewith the harts of all good Christians are affected." The "something" which "gave occasion" to the fatal act has not been ascertained, though it seems clearly established that it was not pecuniary embarassment. Masters, Hist. of Corp. Chr. coll. 141, Append. xliv; Wood's Ath. Oxon. i. 478; Cooper's Annals of Cambr. iii. 251; Smith's Obituary, p. 6. The King's and Queen's visit to Cambridge was on the 22d March, 1631-2. Cooper's Annals, iii. 249.

[b] Henry Sherfield; on this matter see Hatcher's History of Salisbury, fol. 1843, pp. 371-373.

[c] " Histrio-mastix ; the Players' Scourge, or the Actor's Tragedy, in two parts : wherein it is largely evidenced, by divers arguments, that popular stage-plays are sinfull, heathenish, lewde, ungodly spectacles." 4to. London, 1633.

D. C. TO THE GENTLEWOMEN OF THE NEWE DRESSE.[a]

Ladies that weare blacke Cypres vailes,[b]
Turned lately to white linnen railes,[c]
And to your girdle weare your bandes,[d]
And shewe your armes, in steade of handes;
What can you doe in Lent more meet
As, fittest dresse, to weare a sheete?
'Twas once a bande ; 'tis now a cloake ;
An acorne one day proves an oke,
Weare but your linnen to your feete,
And then your band will prove a sheete,
By which devise and wise excesse
You doe a penance in a dresse :
And none shall knowe by what they see,
Which Ladies censur'd, which goe free.

THE LADIES AND GENTLEWOMEN'S ANSWER.

Blacke cypres vailes are shroudes of night,
White linnen vailes are railes of light,[e]
Which, though we to our girdles weare,
W' have handes to keepe your armes of there.
A fitter dresse we have for Lent,
To shewe us truly penitent:
Who makes our bandes to be our cloake
Makes John at Stile of John an Oke.
We weare our linnen to our feete,
Yet need not make our band our sheete :
Your Clergie weare as long as we,
Yet that implies conformity.
Be wise, recant what you have writte,
Least you take [f] penance for your witte.

---

[a] D. C. is Dean Corbet, Bishop of Norwich. This and the following are printed, with slight variations, in the volume entitled " Satirical Songs and Poems on Costume," edited by Mr. Fairholt for the Percy Society, pp. 136, 137. The notes appended are Mr. Fairholt's.           [b] " Cipress was a fine kind of crape or gauze."

[c] " The rayle was the neckerchief."

[d] " Alluding to the great length of the falling band, which was allowed to hang down upon the shoulders."

[e] " White linen railes are raies of light."     Harl. MS. 6,396.

[f] " do penance."     Harl. MS.

Love charmes have power to weave<sup>a</sup> a string
To tye you, as you ty'de your ring.<sup>b</sup>
Thus by love's sharpe but just decree
You may be censurde, we goe free.

UPON SIR THOMAS OVERBURY.—SIR W. R.

Here lies one nowe not worth despising,
Who, Persian-like, worshipt the sun-rising ;
Who, courtier-like, embrac'de the brave,
Now, Lazarus-like, lies in his grave :
Who, stoike-like, contemnde a wife :
God shield hereafter he breed no strife.
Now reade his fate ; though he were brave and bolde,
Yet, like a Jewe, was bought and sould.
Oh bury him, bury him, quoth the high power,
Least he poyson Court, City, and Tower :
And was it not sinne to bury him then
Who living stunke in the face of men !

A LADIE WITH ONE EYE HAD A PRETTY SONNE THAT BY A JERKE OF THE
COACHMAN'S WHIP LOST AN EYE.<sup>c</sup> —JOHN KN.

Thou one-eyed boy, borne of an halfe-blinde mother,
Matchlesse in beuty both, save one to th' other ;
Lend her thy light, sweete ladde, and she shall prove
The Queene of Beuty, thou the God of Love.

---

<sup>a</sup> " weare " in margin and in Harl. MS.

<sup>b</sup> " In a ludicrous ballad, describing James I.'s visit to Oxford in 1621, when Corbet, in his office of chaplain, preached before the King, he is thus spoken of :—

The reverend dean,
With his band starch'd clean,
Did preach before the King;
A ring was his pride,
To his band-strings tied,
Was not this a pretty thing ?

The ring, without doubt,
Was the thing put him out,
And made him forget what was next ;
For every one there
Will say, I dare swear,
He handled it more than his text."

See further stanzas in the Progresses, &c. of James I. iv. 1110.

<sup>c</sup> A copy in Sloane MS. 1792, f. 260, reads thus :—

Fair halfe-blind boy, borne of halfe-blind mother,
Equall'd by none, but by each one the other,
Send her thine eie, sweet boy, and shee shall prove
The Queene of Beauties, thou the God of Love.

A different reading still occurs in Egerton MS. 923, f. 58.

Come faire ladies, come drawe neere, offer here
Unto your maister Crosbie's shrine ;
Breathe one sigh, bestowe one grone on the stone ;
And bath his farewell in your eyne.

Now I have danc'te the measure of my dayes,     *A Dauncer*
And friskte till I am weary, let me rest ;     *about Linn.*
Each honest acte and action serves to praise,
And please the Lord, and I have done my best:

This solitary couch that I have drest
I'le sleepe in, till I shall renewe my yeeres
To dance Lavaltos ᵃ in the highest spheres.

---

La France est disesperée     *The estate of*
Et presque tout ruinée,     *France.*
Par un demon infernal
Que vol ᵇ et qui n'a point d'aisle.
Quan dit tu, Jean de Nivellâ,
C'est Monsieur le Cardinal.

## Returning to Genevah, I made this literall distich,

Glaunce glorious Geneve, Gospell-guiding gem.     *Lithgo.*
Great God, governe good Geneve's ghostly Game.

---

Can Christendome's great Champion sinke away
Thus silently into a bedde of clay ?
Can such a Monarch die, and yet not have     *King of Swe-*
An Earthquake for to open him a grave ?     *den.*
Did there no meteor fright the Universe.
Nor Comet holde a torch unto his herse ?
Was there no clap of Thunder hearde, to tell
All Christendome their losse, and ring his knell ?
Impartiall fates, I see that Princes then,
Though they live gods, yet they must die like men,
And the same passing bell must toll for them
Which rang but nowe the beggar's requiem.
When such a soule is from the earth bereav'ne,
Me thinkes there should be triumphes made in Heaven,
And starres should runne at tilte at his decease,
To welcome him into that place of peace,
Who, though he warred, yet did alwaies strive,
Dying in warre, to leave peace still alive.

---

ᵃ A sort of active bounding waltz.—Halliwell's Dictionary.     ᵇ " Que vole.''

Gustavus Adolphus Rex Suecorum.
Mortuus adhuc Spe salvus exurgo.—

Quem celeri raptum fato, Germania, luges,
   Mortuus exurgo, spe tibi salvus adhuc.

Seeke not, readers, here to finde
Entombde the shroud of such a minde
As did the greate Gustavus fill,
Whom neither time nor death can kill :
Goe and reade the Cæsars' acts,
The rage of Scythian cataracts,
What Epirus, Greece, or Rome
What kingdomes Gothes and Vandals wonne :
Read all the worlde's Heroicke story,
And knowe but halfe this hero's glory.
These conquered living, but life flying
Reviv'de theire foes :  He conquered dying :
And Mars hath offerde, as he falles,
An hecatombe of generalls.
The greate comparer could not tell
Where to drawe out his parallell ;
Then doe not hope to find him here
For whom earth was a narrowe sphere,
Nor, by a search in this small roome,
To find a king above a toombe.

———

'Tis sinne to weep or praise ; oh let me vent
My passion in astonishment.
Who sheddes a teare for the great Swed thus slaine,
His eyes doe penance for his weaker braine,
And yet those eyes themselves deserve this doome,
Which thus mistake a trophe for a toombe.
Or else thy foes may weepe, as then they did
When as thou diedst ; but all their teares were bloud.
Oh what a tempest, what a sea was forc'te
Of tribute grones and sighes, to wafte one ghost !
No way but death they had to flie thy face,
Thou quitt'st thy body to pursue the chace.
But who pretends thy praise, in best expressions,
Endictes his judgment of confest presumptions.
Bolde tongue, touch not that head, that hearte, that hand,
Which brought on's knee, while he did tiptoe stand,
The Pride of Austria backte with all but heaven ;
Himselfe of all but of himselfe bereven.

Thus having plum'de th' Imperiall bird alone,
Upon those eagles' wings to heaven he's flowne.
Why should he stay on earth ? the game is done ;
Others can parte the stake which he hath wonne.
'Tis lowe ambition, underneath his story,
To aime at any crowne but that of glory.
Then canon play, his body's sacrific'de,
He is not canon'd ; no, he's canoniz'de.

Gustavus in the bed of honour dy'de
While victory lay bleeding by his side.

November 16, 1632.

About the newes in Germany, France, and the Lowe Countryes, bookes daily come forth, and the Swedish Intelligencer is come to a fifth parte, &c. This fifth parte came out about St. Andrew.

July the 20, the King returned out of Scotland, having beene lately crowned there. They say there were many pieces, about the bignes of a 9 p. [nine-pence], coined and throwne about at the coronation, by the King and his almoner; having on the one side a thistle, and round about it " Hinc nostræ crevere rosæ." *King Charles returneth out of Scotland to Greenwich.*

Soone after the King's returne, Archbishop Abbot died, and doctor Laud Bishop of London had his place. Doctor Juxton had London, who (*ut dicitur*) was before elect Bishop of Hereford. *Archbishop of Canterbury.*

This summer, Vicount Falkland that had beene Deputy in Ireland being come over, and the Lord Wentworth sent over in his stead, did die miserably at Theobald's. He was neere the King, in a tree or stand, watching to strike a deere, but his foote hold (of the fore foote) brake, and he fell, and brake his legge, so that the marrowe ranne and it was cut of, and seared; but it bledd afresh, and so he soone died, in a day or thereabout. *Cary, Deputy of Ireland.*

October 15, betimes, about 1 in the morning, our King's second sonne James was borne. *Duke James borne.*

In Michaelmas terme, a Jesuite (some say a Dominican Fryer) called Arthur Gohogan, an Irishman, was arraigned at the King's bench barre, and condemned for treason, for that upon shipborde, in an English ship, on the coast of Spain, over against Lisbon, he, discoursing with the marchants about religions and religious states, called our King "heretique," and said if ever he came neere our *Traytor executed.*

King, he wold kill him; and this summer in the end of it, the same merchants (having ij yeeres since talked hereof at theire arrivall in England,) mette him in London, and so discovered it to the councell, &c.   He was executed at Tiburne, alone, (as a cutpurse, taken in the Starre chamber a fewe dayes before, had beene served,) within two dayes.   His quarters and heade being brought to Newgate, there came a letter to bury them, before they were hanged up, so that there was some doubt made where; but at length Mr. Atturny was sent to the King to knowe, and by his advice (for they bury none of us among them, &c.) the carkase was buried under the very place at Tiburne where he was hanged.

**Philip Bushell, innocent.**
**Irish Judge censured, &c.**
November 27, was censured the Lord Vicount Kilmallock, chief justice of the Common pleas in Ireland, Sir Henry Bealings, and one Pilsworth, about the death of Philip Bushell in Ireland, who was hanged nine or ten yeeres since.   A notable case, which I heard and have penned in a folio paper booke: Foure men, robbers of houses and otherwise, who before were saved and sent for soldiers, but leaving theire colours and returning to theire former course, were hanged on four severall gibbets, erect for the time at four gates of London, December 7, or thereabouts.

**Woman burned.**
A woman was burned in Smithfield December 13, who, in a falling-out with her husband, stabbed him in the necke with a knife; so that, following her downe a payer of stayers, and crying out to stay her, he died at the bottome of them immediatly.

Bishop Bayly died this terme.

**Sabbath sports.**
The King's booke for Sabath recreations came forth a litle before.[a]
**Sope-boyling.**
After much adoe about sope-boyling, which had beene long on
**King's Atturny dieth.**
foote, &c.[b]   Mr. Atturny Generall, William Noye, died about August 1634.

**Farthings callde in.**
Farthings of brasse were this spring called in by a printed proclamation or order from the councell table, whereby it was ordered

---

[a] "The King's Majesty's Declaration to his Subjects, concerning Lawful Sports to be used." 4to. London, 1633.   Reprinted in Harl. Miscell. vol. x. p. 75.

[b] A proclamation about soap-boiling, &c. settling former disputes, dated 13th July, 1634, is printed in Fœdera, vol. viii. pt. iv. p. 83.

that no labourer &c. should be paid with farthings, and that no man should dare to offer above ij of them in any summe, and that they are to serve in exchange, no man being charged to receive j. of them. The country had beene formerly abused with whole barrels of false farthings brought in among them.

The Protestants in Germany received this summer a greate over- throwe. qu?

*Protestants overthrowne.*

Michaelmas terme. The Lord Heath [a] (common pleas) being dis- placed, sir John Finch is in his roome.

*Lord Heath. Sir John Finch.*

Sir John Bankes made Atturny. Mr. Recorder Littleton [b] is *(ut dicitur)* the King's Sollicitor, and the knight(?) made Serjeant.

*Atturney.*

Doctor Lushington, at Norwich, after his sermon to the trayners, gave out these verses.

### NISI DOMINUS.

Skill, Number, Courage cannot prosper us
Without our posie, Nisi Dominus.
The strongest cities have [c] been ominous
To theire owne keepers, Nisi Dominus.
And every stone to the towne and us
May prove a bullet, Nisi Dominus,
The gunne or sticke may make a piteous [d]
And bloody muster, Nisi Dominus.
Since power and skill in armes be governd thus
We dare say nothing, Nisi Dominus.

MAXIME PONTIFEX,[e]

Domus Lotharingica, olim modoque principum regumque mater, vincula trahit dura et in captivitatem ducitur, orbe spectante et dolente. Sanguis mihi (optime pontifex) in venis salit, quem ex domo Lotharingicâ hausi, pulsat-

---

[a] Sir Robert Heath. See Court and Times of Charles I., vol. ii. p. 137, and see also his biography in the first volume of the Miscellany of the Philobiblon Society.

[b] Sir Edward Littleton, afterwards chief justice of the Common Pleas.

[c] " Rather *had* " in margin.          [d] " Piteous indeed " in margin.

[e] The name of the author of this letter is not given, but internal evidence points it out as the production of Gaston Duke of Orleans, brother of Louis XIII. He married, in 1632, Margaret of Lorraine, sister of the dukes Charles and Nicolas Francis. This alliance brought down upon the house of Lorraine the wrath of Louis XIII., who was at variance with his brother, and in 1634 duke Charles was self-exiled in Germany, and duke Nicolas, in whose behalf he had abdicated, was languishing in prison at Nanci.

que vehementer metus ipsa præcordia, dum consanguineos meos duces, patriis sedibus spoliatos, intueor, et hostilia graviter passos. Sanguis cum in nobis idem sit, est etiam et amor ; distrahor tamen affectibus ; hinc cognati Lotharingiæ oppressi jacent, inde frater meus triumphatur ; sed et illorum calamitati violenta si manu faveam, necesse erit hunc ut vulnerem. Itaque utrinque amore cogor ad mediationes aliorum principum confugere, ut amicitiam inter hos mihi charos conciliem, bella amore extinguem, non aliter sane extinguenda nisi fœdâ sanguinis Christiani effusione. Ad te ergo, Urbane Pontifex, quem omnis humanitatis cultu ut optimum principem semper suspexi, potissimum mihi, inter alios principes, confugiendum existimavi, quod hi principes potestatem tuam videantur perfecte agnoscere, se oves, teque pastorem, pastorem suum. Impera igitur (sanctitatem tuam ita obtestor) hisce tuis filiis, patris ut sui vocem audientes armis sepositis, pacem Christianam ineant cæterisque principibus authoritatem tuam agnoscentibus exemplo sint. Deponatur, te sedente pacifico et potente, quodcumque inter illos violentum, sedeturque. Reddantur hæreditati suæ cognati duces, cæterique Lotharingiæ domûs principes reponantur in avitas sedes. Hoc si jubeat tua in illos potentia, curabit procul dubio paterna manus filiorum tuorum vulnera, prædicabitque Christianis orbis, ab Urbano Pontifice Romano, domum Lotharingicam, ex quâ pœne orti omnes Christiani principes, flori donari pristino, et vitæ restitui. Tot vero inter reges et principes qui Christianam hanc domum matrem agnoscant, ego Urbano principi optimo, unà cum illis, gratias immortales agam, quodque huic domui parenti meæ a sanctitate tua præstabitur, tanquam mihimet meisque coronis præstitum, grato animo semper agnoscam ; et fatendum est nihil mihi gravius contigisse quam optimæ illius domûs, mihique conjunctissimæ, contemplari ruinam.

---

### THE NEW CHURCHMAN.

1635.

> A ceremonious, light-timbred scholler,
> With a little dam-mee [a] peeping over his coller ;
> With a Cardinal's cap, broad as a carte wheele,
> With a long coate and cassocke down to his heele.
>     See a newe Churchman of the times,
>         O the times, the times' newe Churchman !
>
> With long haire and a shorte grace,
> Which, being sharpe set, he snaps up apace,
> And after dinner, such a little touch—
> His belly is so full he cannot say much.    See, &c.

---

[a] " Dammy, from the soldier's band, who usually sweareth God dam me." in margin.

His gravity rides up and downe,
In a long coate or a shorte gowne ;
And sweares, by the halfe football on his pate,
That no man is predestinate.  See, &c.

His Divinity is trust up with five points,
He dops, ducks, bowes, as made all of joints ;
But when his Romane nose standes full East,
He feares neither God nor beast.  See, &c.

He hopes to be saved by prevision
Of good workes, but will doe none ;
He will be no Protestant, but a Christian,
And comes out Catholike the next edition.  See, &c.

Some halfe-dozen of benefices gone downe his gullet,
Yet he gapes as though his belly were not full yet ;
And sure his Curate must be turned away,
If he chance to preach twice a day.  See, &c.

On fasting nights, he hath a collation ;
And on Sundayes, a great preparation
Of cardes, dice, and high joviality,
And all to confute the formality.  See, &c.

Many of these rimes came out in these late times, about 1634 and See the next page. 1635, on both sides, some against the orthodoxe, others against these " newe churchemen," &c.

1635 came out Shelford's " Five pious and learned Discourses," &c. Printed by the printers to the University of Cambridge.  A booke neither pious nor learned, written by one [a] wholly savouring of the spirit of Antichrist, and ignorant of the maine scope of the Gospell, &c.

November 13, 1635.  I sawe a booke entitled " God's Love to Mankind manifested, by disprooving his absolute decree for theire damnation.  Hose, 13, 9.  Wisdome, 1, 12, 13.  Imprinted anno Domini 1635."

In October, Doctor Stoughton,[b] of Aldermanbury, in London, who *Mary Aldermanbury.*

---

[a] Robert Shelford was of Peterhouse.   The Puritans loudly complained of Dr. Beale the Vice-chancellor for licensing Shelford's Discourses.  Cooper, Annals of Cambridge, iii. 268.

[b] John Stoughton, D.D., sometime fellow of Emmanuel College, died 4 May, 1639. (Smith's Obituary, p. 16.)   A brief notice of him and his works is given in Brook's Lives of the Puritans, iii. 527.

had married Cudworth's widowe, of Emm.[a] and had the same living given by the colledge in the West country, from whence a carrier bringing some monyes for his wives children's portions, he was traduced (as it seemeth) to be a favourer of New England, and a collector of contribution for those ministers there, &c.: so that a pursevant was sent to the carrier, and many halbard-men for him and his study was sealed up, &c.: but within 2 or 3 dayes, *re cognitâ*, he returned with credite, in the earl of Holland's coach.

1636.　In 1636 came forth a booke (said to be Doctor Heylen's)[b] called "A Coale from the Altar;" indeede a confutation of an epistle of the Bishop of Lincolne to the Vicar of Grantham, about the placing of the communion table. The same was answered by the bishop's approbation 1637. This yeere many were troubled and suspended, about the ceremonies enquired of in the articles of Bishop Wren, in his diocesse of Norwich.[c] This yeere was doctor Juxton, Bishop of London, made Lord Treasurer of England.

See the former page. These following verses[d] came to men's hands in these times.

| | |
|---|---|
| I hold as faith | What England Church allowes |
| What Rome Church saith | My conscience disallowes. |
| Where the King is head | That church can have no shame |
| That folke is misled | That holdeth Pope supreme. |
| Where the altar is drest | Their service is scarce divine |
| The people are blest | With table, bread, and wine. |
| He is but an asse | Who the Communion flies |
| That shunnes the Masse | Is Catholike and wise. |

---

[a] Ralph Cudworth, B.D., sometime fellow of Emmanuel College, Cambridge, died rector of Aller in Somersetshire, in August or September 1624. He was the father of the famous divine of the same name, who died 26 June, 1688, having been successively fellow of Emmanuel College, Master of Clare Hall, and Master of Christ's College.

[b] Peter Heylin. "A Coal from the Altar, or an Answer to Dr. G. Williams's Letter to the Vicar of Grantham, against the placing of the Communion Table at the East end of the church. Lond, 1637."　　　[c] See Clarendon's History, vol. ii. p. 135.

[d] These verses were obviously intended to be read in a double sense; that is, as they appear, or thus,

I hold as faith What Rome Church saith, &c.

See Collet's Relics of Literature (a work really written by Tho. Byerley), pp. 169, 170.

Towardes the ende of August, newes came of bonefires at West-minster, Lambeth (London was under God's visitation of the plague), and the Tower ordinance let of, for joy of our gracious King's deliver-ance; who (*ut dicitur*) in progresse, and riding in a forest alone, fell into a bog, with his horse and himselfe up to the chinne, in greate danger; but by chance a stranger comming by saved him, to whom he gave ij. pieces, and promised 100 li. annuat.

The Palsgrave hath beene here, and continueth here yet.

The newes is that an army (the king of France being in Navarre, for recovery of it) of Savoians, Burgundians, Loreiners, Spaniards, and Imperialists, have forraged and burnte the hether parte of France, and are possessed of Paris and Orleance; the French nobility favour-ing this, in distaste of theire king, upon discontents. This larum was in greate part false; only they foraged, as it is likely, thereby to drawe the French king from Navarre.

A greate plague remained till November, when 800 in a weeke died at London; Michaelmas terme put of.

A very sore winde November 4, in the evening or forpart of the night, which overturned many milles, splitte and sunke two barges, and drowned the men, as they were to Lynne-ward. It did questionles exceeding much harme; Licham [a] burnt that night.

The Swedes obteined a great victory against the duke of Saxony and the Imperialists. The duke's horse saved him by his swiftnes. Seventy ensignes taken; many thousands slaine. The fight lasted many dayes.

The Palsgrave and his brother earle Robert (Rupert) departed out of England about midsommer.

The plague remained, since the last yeere, in London, and there died, about July 7, 180 or thereabout in a weeke. It was sore in Newcastle the last yeere, and remaines there still, as is said. It was at Hadley [b] sore this summer, and at Bury it began to increase, so that July there died 30 in a weeke.

<hr/>

[a] Litcham, hundred of Launditch, co. Norfolk.          [b] Hadleigh, co. Suffolk.

League.

A league is talked of, about June 24, to be made offensive and defensive, betweene England, France, Holland, Swedeland, Denmarke. The Emperor Ferdinand died 1636; of the newe Emperor, see in the Palsgrave's manifesto.

Mr Burton, Dr. Bastwick, Mr. Prin, censured.

Mr. Burton, preacher of Fryday Street, London, Doctor Bastwicke and Mr. Prin, were censured in the Starre-chamber; Mr. Burton for ij. sermons upon Proverbs, Feare God, honor the King, &c., wherein he came to charge the bishops (whom he termed prelates), especially the archbishop and bishop of Norwich, with diverse particuler irregularities, and also for seeking innovation and a secret introducing of Popery. There had beene diverse seditious bookes printed, as "Newes from Ipswich," &c. whereof they were accused. The cen-

At Westminster.

sure was executed the Friday after Trinity terme. Mr. Burton and Doctor Bastwicke lost their eares, and Mr. Prin, who had lost his before for Histriomastix, was branded on both cheekes with S. L. slanderous libeller.[a] Theire further censure was to be imprisoned in three severall castles, farre disseevered, where no hope of comming together, and to be kept without pen, inke, or paper, during their lives. About Moonday, July 9, the Lord Williams, Bishop of

Bishop of Lincolne censured.

Lincolne, was censured in the Starre-chamber, to pay to a knight, against whom he had suborned a witnesse, 1,000 marke, to the

Hook or crook.

prosecutor 100 marke, to the King 10,000li., for unseemly wordes, and to be imprisoned at the King's pleasure; to be deprived of all his dignities, and left to the high commission courte for other matters. (*Sic dicitur.*) He was once parson of Hunnington,[b] or curate there, neere Ixworth in Suffolk. He was lord keeper.

Breda beleguered and besieged by the Hollanders.

Breda was by a fine stratageme besieged with advantage. The

[a] Full particulars of the proceedings against them were published in a pamphlet entitled "A new discovery of the Prelates' tyranny, in their late prosecutions of Mr. William Pryn, an eminent lawyer, Dr. John Bastwick, a learned physician, and Mr. Henry Burton, a reverend divine," &c. 4to. London, 1641. See also Rushworth, pt. ii. vol. i. pp. 324, 380-5, and Clarendon's History, vol. i. p. 292. Burton's sermons are entitled "For God and the King;" not as the diarist has quoted the title. They were 5th November sermons, preached from Proverbs, xxiv, 22, 23.

[b] Honington, Blackburn hundred, co. Suffolk.

Hollanders made a great shewe with a navy over against Flanders, untill the Don Car.[a] had drawne out of Breda and other places a great power to attend or prevent theire attempt; then, on the suddaine, they stole up the river unto Breda, and presently begirte it, July or thereabout.   Taken about Michaelmas.[b]          Taken.

Bury sore visited with the plague; begunne about midsommer.   Norwich a litle.   *March* 1, 1637, *it removed.*[b]

A gentleman named                         ,[c] of 500li. annuat., a yonger   Reporte true
brother, Adams, an high constable of 100 annuat. and one other,   for the generall.
were hanged at Bedford.   They had many confederates and attendants.   They had robbed diverse yeeres altogether between sunne and sunne (so the hundreds were sued), and tooke great summes, 200, 300li. at a time.   They were about in diverse shires, Essex, Suffolk, Lincolnshire, Yorkeshire, Cambridgeshire, Hartfordshire, Buckingham, Northampton, &c.   The gentleman was hanged by sunne-rise, brought in a coache, *ut dicitur.*

The greate ship (Edgar) lanched, August 1637; so many tunnes   Ship.
burthen, besides ordinary carriage.

An extraordinary embassador, with rich presents from the king   October.
of Morocco and Fesse; our ships had helped him to take Sally, a towne of pirates.[d]

> Twas said [f] that Ceremonious Bucke          Mr. Bucke [e] of
>     Had got the presentation          Stradbrooke,
> Of Wilby, Jermy, 'twas ill lucke,          Suffolk.
>     'Twas but a sequestration.

---

[a] Don Carlos de Colonna, general of the Spanish forces in the Netherlands.

[b] Added later.          [c] Blank in MS.

[d] John Dunton, one of the expedition, published " A true journal of the Sally fleet, with the proceedings of the voyage." 4to. London, 1637.   Sallee was a town in Barbary, in the hands of the Moors, who ten years before revolted against the Emperor of Morocco, and, forming themselves into a republic, entreated help from England, and offered the subjection of the place to Charles I.; but he took the other side in the quarrel.   In Additional MS. 15,226, f. 57, is the letter from the King of Morocco to Charles I., sent on this occasion.   Court and Times of Charles I., vol. i. pp. 243, 255.

[e] James Buck, B.D., a determined Episcopalian and Loyalist.   For an account of him see Davy's Suffolk Collections, Additional MS. 19,092, f. 262.   He was sequestered by Parliament in 1643.

[f] " *Saint* for ' said ' was the author's word " in margin.

Had Bucke the maister beene prefer'de,
    As fame reporteth sure,
Jermy had beene the journyman,
    And should have servde the cure.
But see the lucke ; unluckie Bucke
    Stickes fast and cannot drawe ;
And Balle[a] shall eate the provender,
    Whilste Bucke doth champe the strawe.
Whilste Bucke's preferd beyond the seas,
    Jermy may stand and cry,
With whip and lash most carter-like,
    And whistle " hie, Bucke, hie."
'Twas said young Warner Wilby had,
    And he should rector be,
But that he was too young a lad,
    To rule a rectory.
Then it was said pure Turnball should
    In steade of him succeed ;
And many sisters were in hope
    That he should have't indeed.
But see the lucke that Balle should turne,
    And so be brought about
That famous Balle of Penbroke hall
    Should turne pure Turnball out.
But if Balle be beyond the seas,
    As nowe report doth goe,
Then may we doe as carters use,
    Even whistle " Ho, Ball, ho."

March 19. Some yeeres since I saw in Holborne, London, neere the bridge (my brother there), an Italian, who with his mouth did lay certaine sheetes of paper together, one upon another lengthwise, betweene the right hand and the left; and then he **Italian sight.** tooke a needle and prickte it through the one ende, and so then the other, so that the paper lay sure. Then he tooke a shorte texte pen, and dipped it in a standish or inkehorne of leade, and therewith wrote *Laus Deo semper*, in a very fayer text hand (not writter

---

[a] Dr. Richard Ball, rector of Wilby and Westerfield, co. Suffolk, afterwards chaplain of Charles II. See an account of him ibid. f. 372.

with his hand but his mouth); then with another pen he florished
daintily about these letters in diverse formes.  He did with his
mouth also take up a needle and threed, pricking the needle right
down, out of which he puld the threed, and tooke another by (fitted),
and put it into the needle.  Then therewith he tooke three stitches
in a cloathe with a linnen-wheele (prepared with a turner's devise
for the foote).  He did spin with his mouth.  He wrote fayer with
his left foote.  He used a pensill and painted with his mouth.  He
tooke a pretty piece or gun with his toes, and poured in a paper of
poulder, pulled out the skouring sticke very nimbly, rammed in the
poulder, put up the sticke, puld up the cocke with his toes; then
another short piece charged (that had a Swedish firelocke), being
put in his mouth by another man, he held it forth and discharged
it, and forthwith with his toes he discharged the other.  He
gathered up four or five small dice with his foote, and threw them
out featly.  His hands were both shrimped and lame.

The Scottish troubles on foote.

The Fennes in some townes remaine still.

Dividing of Commons.

Shipmony determined for the King by his prerogative, argued
Easter and Trinity terme.

In Michaelmas terme, the lord Saye brought his action about
it to the King's bench barre.  Mr. Holborne, pleading strongly for
him, was rebuked by judge Bartlet; [a] because it was determined as
before, he alledged a president when such determinings have been
againe questioned.  Judge Crooke alledged presidents.  Judge Joanes
said they were not like.  Sir Jo. Brampton alledged that they had
no president like this, viz. to call the thing in question the next
terme, and before the judges' faces that did determine it.  The lord
Saye affirmed, that, if theire lordships wold say it were lawe, then
he wold yeeld; but otherwise not, to the wronging of his country.
He hath time to consider untill the next terme.

[a] Sir Robert Berkeley.

Tubbing lost one eare at Westminster, and, ere he lost the other in Norfolk, he died in prison at London.

Many great censures in the Starre-chamber. Tubbing. The jur; found 10,000 damages against Mr. Harrison, clerk, Northampton for charging judge Hutton with treason openly in Westminster hall about the ship mony (*ut dicitur*).

Prince Robert, or erle Rupert, and the lord Craven taken prisoners, and the Palgrave hardly escaping.

Feare of warres from Scotland, except theire assemblie quiet all It was (*ut dicitur*) Wednesday, November 21. God can deliver us from these feares! Armor prepared. Sir Jacob Astley and diverse captaines attending at court. About Swafham Priory and Botson,[a] the enclosures were throwne downe and the cattell turnd in to feed as before. The mad-shavers women abused a woman inhumanely. The Scottish busines on foote requires a volume to relate and time to prepare for it.

ON THE KING OF FRANCE HIS STATUE ON HORSEBACKE IN BRASSE AT NANTES,
BY ARMANDAS RICHELIEU.

Sta, quisquis es;
Reverere hunc regem, si subditus es;
Mirare, si externus; metue, si injustus.
Hic est Ludovicus decimus tertius.
Natus est cum justitiâ,
dum Sol nasceretur in Libra,
Sed sæpe sol libram, nunquam æquitatem
Ludovicus deseruit.
Hæc equitas eum Europæ judicem fecit et vindicem :
Hoc vindice,
Rhætia in hostium casses non incidit;
Sabaudiæ verruca una non periit;
Cassale, ter oppugnatum, non cecidit.
Hunc arbitrum
si Germania elegisset,
et libertatem retineret
et religionem;
et si neutra esse voluisset,
utraque esset.

---

[a] Boston.

Fortitudinem ex victoria collige :
Infra Galliæ regnum alterum superavit,
dum Rupellibus trecentas arces eripuit.
Omnia Rupellæ elementa vicit;
Ignem aquis,
Terram vallis,
Aerem carcere,
Oceanum aggere.
Stetit ad hunc aggerem Anglus
ubi Oceanus steterat :
ter ad Rupellam victus est solo aspectu,
ter ad Cassale Hispanus,
semel etiam non aspectus,
Pignerolium domitarum Alphium trophæum
toti Europæ testatur
quid ultra Alpes agere potuisset Ludovicus,
nisi propugnator libertatis Italicæ
quam expugnator esse voluisset.
Nantium Galliæ voluit,
ne Gotheræ esset;
et ne unquam esset inimica,
eligit esse subdita.
Mola solo nomine immobilem esse jactavit,
at expugnata est;
ne quid armis Ludovici immobile esset.
Hæc si miracula videntur,
hoc sæculo perpetrata,
prævidit etiam ab altero seculo
Clemens Octavus;
meditatur majora :
Armandus Richelicus
interea Ludovico justo et victori
hanc armatam statuam
humilis et gratus posuit.        A. R. C. E.

The 27 of March, 15 Car. 1639, his Majestie rode through Scottish trou-
Roiston to Yorke-ward, there to meete his army, &c.   It was told bles. King
me, April 1, that whereas it is an use to deliver billes for the sicke Charles goeth towards Scot-
to be praid for in this manner; one from the church dore perhaps land.
in the throng pulles another by the shoulder, and gives him the note
or bill, he another, &c., untill it come to [the] clerke; the clerke,

at the preacher's comming into the pulpit, delivers them to him, &c
Some one had put up a bill which the preacher wold not reade, but
let it fall.   The bill *(ut dicitur)* was thus: " John Commonwealth's-
man of Great Britaine, being sicke of the Scottish disease, desires
the prayers of this congregation for a parliament."

On Thursday, August the 1, the King returned from Barwicke,
&c.   The Palsgrave, lately arrived, had gone to him, and returned
with him.   The lord of Arundell, lord generall, returned somewhile
before.   The campe brake up a month before.

Aprill 13.   A parliament was assembled anno 1640, but forthwith dissolved.   The warres were prosecuted and renued against
Scotland.   Much discontent.   Insurrections at London.   Insolen-
cies by souldiers.   The lord Loudon, of Scotland, imprisoned.[a]
Ship mony exacted, and in diverse places diversly refused.   Much
troble feared on the seas by reason of diverse shippes on our coastes.
The Queen neere deliverance.   A fast ordeined July 8, &c.

ON THE DISSOLUTION OF THE SHORT PARLIAMENT OF 1640.

[b] Two parliaments dissolv'de ! then let my heart
As they in factions, it in fractions part;
And, like the Levite, sende with griefe a scribe,
My peece-mealde portion [c] to eche broken tribe;
And say that Bethlem Judah's love have [d] been
Wrongde by the fagge-end crue [e] of Benjamin.
Oh let such high presumption be accurst,
When the last tribe shall wrong the best and first;
When, like the Levite, our best Charles may say,
" The ravenous wolfe hath seisde the lion's preye."
Thus oft inferior subjects are not shie,
To wrong the love that rests in majestie.[f]

Margin notes: John Commonwealth's man. King Charles returneth. Of this Scottish busines many bookes, writings, and records are to be had. 1640.

[a] He was at the head of the covenanting lords.   He was committed to the private custody of one of the sheriffs of London.   (Rushworth, pt. ii. vol. ii. p. 1103.)
[b] Collated with a copy in Harl. MS. 367, f. 160.
[c] " And, like the Levite, sad with rage ascribe
Its pecemele portions," &c.   Harl. MS.
[d] " hath."          [e] " fagg and cryes."
[f] " To wrong alone, but mocke at majestie."

What faults, what injuries shold not be mended,[a]
If that the feet had power to spurne the head?
And kings' prerogatives must needes fall downe,
When subjects make a footeball of the crowne.
The starres (the heaven's inferior courtiers) might
Command the darknes, but not rule the light,
Nor him that makes it; shold they all combine,
With Luna at the full, one sun wold shine
Brighter then they; nor can he be subdu'de,
Though he but one, and they a multitude.
Say, subjects, you were starres, and 'twere allowed,
You justly of your number might be proude;
Yet to the sunne be humble, and know this,
Your light is borrowed—not your owne, but his.
When the unfettered subjects of the seas,
The fountaines, felt their silver feet had ease,
No sooner summonde, but they nimbly went,
To meet the ocean at a parliament.
Did then these petty fountaines say theire king,
An ocean, was no ocean, but a spring?
Let me alone, if fresher newes of store[b]
Doe make me porer than I was before.
And shall we then the power of kings dispute,
And count it lesse when more is added too 't?
No; let the common body, if it can,
Be not a river, but an ocean,
And swell into a deluge, till it hide
The toppes of mountaines in its teeming pride;
Kings, like Noah's arke, are neerer to the skies,
The more the billowes under them doe rise.
You then, who, if your hearts be fired with love,
Might sit in counsell, like the gods with Jove;
You that doe question the King's power below,
If you come there, will you use Heaven's King so?
Do not aspire; you may, taking your rest,
More safer be belowe then in the eagle's nest.
Hath clemency offended, and [c] will you harme,
And plucke the sun from Heaven that makes you warme?

---

a " What facultie should not be injured."
b "fresh access of store."　　　　　　　　　c " and " omitted.

CAMD. SOC.　　　　N

No King, no Bishop ! please ? what have we gott?
An outside English and an inside Scott ?
If faction thus our countrie's peace distracts,
We may have wordes of parliaments, not acts.
Ill-ended sessions ! and yet well begun ;
Too much being spoke hath made too little done :
For factions thrive, puritanisme sway,[a]
None must doe any thing, but only say.
Stoop downe, you barren-headed hilles, confesse
You might be fruitfull if that you were lesse.
Tremble, you threadbare commons; are you vext
That lambes feed on you ? lions will come next.

FINIS.

Justice Crooke argued April 14, 1638, in the Exchequer Chamber [the case of ship-money] before all the judges of England and Barons of the Exchequer.[b]

**Insurrections and tumults.**

Mr. Prinne's speech to the lower house of parliament.[c]

Upon the dissolving of the parliament,[d] presently were two insurrections in one weeke, at Southwarke and Lambeth; in the first the White Lion pryson was broken and prisoners set free, &c.; in the second, Lambeth House in hazard, &c. One man was taken and hanged and quartered ; see a proclamation about it.

This summer, by reason of billeting of soldiers, many outrages were done. In Barkeshire, captaine Mohun (Moone) was slaine, and basely and inhumanely used, being at last hanged up on an old pillory. There is a proclamation against 600 of this company about Faringdon in Berkeshire, neere Oxfordshire, thirteen principall. A like proclamation there is about stirres in Somersetshire by about 120, &c.

[a] " Puritans bear sway."
[b] Rushworth, pt. ii. vol. ii. App. pp. 177-212.
[c] Printed in Rushworth, pt. ii. vol. ii. pp. 1131-1136.            [d] May 5, 1640.

The humble Petition of the gentry in your Majesties county of Yorke, now Petitions deli-
assembled at the assises of Yorke, this 28 day of July, 1640.[a]        vered, or intended *(ut*
*dicitur)*.

TO THE KING'S MOST EXCELLENT MAJESTIE.[b]

The humble Petition of your Majesties loyall subjects the Grand Jury,
empanelled the 11th of July, 1640, to serve at the generall assises holden for
the county of Berkes, in the behalfe of themselves and the rest of the
bodie of the county: Sheweth,

That whereas your Petitioners have been of late yeeres, and still are, much
burthened with sundry greevances of diverse natures, deriving theire authority from your Majestie, but being directly contrary to your Majesties lawes
established in this your kingdome, the chiefe of them presenting themselves in
a schedule hereunto annexed, for redresse whereof, as your Petitioners hoped,
your Majestie was graciously pleased, about the middle of April last, to
assemble the great councell, commonly called the high court of Parliament, and
some three weekes after to dissolve the same, for want (as it seemes to your
Petitioners) of a good agreement betwixt the two houses ; and nevertheles,
since the said dissolution, to expresse such a fatherly care of your pore
people, that your Majestie hath vouchsafed, by your printed Declaration, to
invite them to the pouring out of theire complaints into your princely eare :—

It may, therefore, please your most excellent Majestie to take the said particulers into your tender consideration, and to give your Petitioners such ease
therein as in your royall wisedome shall be fitte ; and whereby it may appeere
to all your Majesties subjects, especiallie to those of your Majesties most
honourable privy counsell, and the other officers and ministers of justice, that
you are resolved to continue to them all theire rights and liberties, which they
desired by the Petition of Right, and were confirmed by your Majestie in the
third yeer of your reigne ; and your petitioners, as most bound, shall continue
to procure the length and happines of your Majesties said reigne by theire
prayers and all actions of zeale and duty.

---

[a] Printed with variations in Rushworth, pt. ii. vol. ii. p. 1214.
[b] Collated with a copy in Harl. MS. 4931, f. 129.        [c] " desired."

A SCHEDULE OF SUCH GREEVANCES AS MOST OPPRESSE THIS COUNTRY.

1. The illegall and unsupportable charge of Ship-mony, nowe the fifth yeere imposed as high as ever, though the subject was not able to pay the last yeer, being a third.

2. The newe taxe of Coate and Conduct Mony, with undue meanes used to inforce the payment of it, by messengers from the Counsell table.

3. The compelling some free-men, by imprisonment and threatnings, to take Presse-mony; and others, for feare of the like imprisonment, to forsake theire place of habitation, hiding themselves in woods, whereby theire families are left to the charge of the parish, and harvest worke undone for want of labourers.

4. The infinite number of Monopolies upon every thing the countryman must buy.

Besides the easterne parte of this county, where your Majesties forrest of Windsor is particularly burthened:

1. With the unmeasurable increase of the deere, which, if they should goe on so for a few yeares more, will leave neither food nor roome for any other creature in the forrest.

2. With the rigid execution of the forrest lawes in theire extremity.

3. With the exaction of immoderate fees by some officers under the Lord Chief Justice in Eyre.

Newcastle surprised by the Scottes.

About the 27 or 29 of August, Newcastle-upon-Tine was surprised by the Scottes, his Majestie being neere it, and our armie before it. In the surprisall, we lost some horse and men. The surprisall was without slaughter in the towne, and the possession without pillage (*ut dicitur*); what the event will be, God alone knoweth. Let us in loyalty pray for an happie ende of these troubles, with his Majestie's long happines in the quiet of his kingdomes! Amen.

Three proclamations.

His Majestie had lately 3 proclamations, dated August 20; 1, for the Shipmony, with all former arrerages to be paid by the 20 of October next.[a] 2, for all holding of the King by Grand Serjeantie, Escuage,

---

[a] Fœdera, vol. ix. pt. iii. p. 26.

Knight-service, to attend the King at the campe royall, at Newcastle or elsewhere in the North, with horses, &c. by September 20; or else to compound with commissioners appointed at London, by the same day.[a]   3, for to make knowne that certaine Scottes in hostile manner had invaded the land, and to proclaime those that were come and those that should come in traitors, with all their abbettors and relievers, &c.

The humble Petition of your Majesties most loyall subjects, whose names are here underwritten, in behalfe of themselves and many others.[b]    Received September 9.

Most Gracious Soveraigne,

The speed of that suite[c] and service which we owe to your Majestie, and our ernest affection to the good and welfare of your Realme of England, hath moved us, in all humility, to beseech your Royal Majestie to give us leave to offer to your princely wisedome the apprehension which we and others of your faithfull subjects have conceived, of the great distemper and danger now threatening the Church and State and your royal person, and of the fittest meanes by which they may be removed and prevented.

The evill and dammages whereof your Majestie may be pleased to take notice are,—

That your Majesties sacred person is exposed to hazard and danger in the present expedition against the Scottes' armie, and by the occasion of this warre your revenues much wasted, your subjects much burthened with coate and conducte money, billiting of soldiers raised for that service, and your whole kingdome become full of care and discontent.

The sundry innovations in matters of religion, the oath and canons lately imposed upon the clergie and other your Majesties subjects, the great increase of popery and employing of popish recusants and others evill affected to your religion, by lawe established, in places of power and trust, especially in commanding men and armes, both in the field and in sundry countries of this your

---

[a] Ibid. vol. ix. pt. iii. p. 27.

[b] Printed with differences in Rushworth, pt. ii. vol. ii. p. 1262 ; but the present is the better copy.   The signatures marked with an asterisk are not in Rushworth, which on the other hand gives "earl of Bristol" and "Pagett," which are not in the MS., nor in a contemporaneous copy in Sloane MS. 1467, f. 132.

[c] "The sense of that duty."

realme, whereas by the lawes they are permitted to have no armes in theire owne houses.  The greate mischiefe which may fall upon this kingdome, if the intention which hath credibly been reported, of bringing in Irish and forreine forces, should take effect.  The urging of shipmony, and prosecution of sheriffes in the Starre Chamber for not levying it.

The heavie charges upon merchandise, to the discouraging of trade.  The multitude of monopolies, and other patents, whereby the commodities and manufactures of this kingdome are much burthened, to the great and universall greevance of your people.

The great griefe of the subjects by the long intermission of parliaments, and the late and former dissolving of such as have been called, without the happie effect which otherwise they might have produced.

Remedy.

For remedie whereof, and the prevention of danger which may ensue to your royall person and the whole state :—

They doe, in all humility and faithfulness, beseech your most excellent Majestie, that you wold be pleased to summon a parliament, within some shorte and convenient time, whereby the cause of those and other great greevances which your people lie under may be taken away, and the authors and councellors of them may be brought to such legall tryall and condigne punishment as the nature of theire severall offences shall require, and the present warre may be composed by your wisedome, without effusion of bloud, in such manner as may conduce to the honor and safetie of your Majesties person, the comfort of your people, and the unity of both your realmes against common enemies of reformed religion.

And your Majesties Petitioners shall alwaies pray, &c.

| Earles. | Earles. | Vicounts. | Barons. |
|---|---|---|---|
| BEDFORD, | BULLINGBROOKE. | SAY AND SEALE. | * LORD NORTH. |
| HERTFORD. | * RUTLAND. | MANDEVILL. | * WILLOUGHBY. |
| ESSEX. | * LINCOLNE. | LORD BROOKE. | * SAVILE. |
| MIDGRAVE. [a] | * EXCETER. | LORD HOWARD. | * WHARTON. |
| WARWICKE. | | | * LOVELACE. |

'Tis said by some that this petition was made by xij nobles, erle of Warwicke, lord Say, &c.   Some say that the councell did joine, excepting, &c.   Others say that some of the privy councell under-

---

[a] " Mulgrave," Rushworth ; " Musgrave," Sloane MS. 1467, f. 132 b.

tooke the delivery of it.　But it is reported (as materiall if true) that his Majestie enclineth, and that commissioners are appointed to treate with the Scottes (who be advancing) upon the 10th of this September.　There is also a reporte that the Scottes, being willing to referre all to an English parliament, doe affirme that if his Majestie dare not trust a parliament in Scotland, nor yet in England, that he is but in evill case.

About the month of July, there was a projecte on foote for brasse- *Brasse-mony.* mony.　It was solemnly debated, as may hereby appeere:—

Whether it be for his Majesties service to coine brasse mony, and make the same currant within his dominions.

The two considerable points in all things doe in this eminently fall into consideration, viz. honor and profit.

For point of honor, it hath alwaies been helde a point of high *Honor.* reputation to kings and monarches to keepe their standerdes certaine, and not to change them, as states and republikes have sometimes done, to supply present necessity, and some princes likewise; though all of them have found the issue of such remedies worse then the disease.

It is more honor for a prince to have all his rules and ordinances knowne and certaine, then changeable, and to direct them to the good of his subjects, though with his owne losse, rather then to use his power to gaine advantage to himselfe, with the prejudice of his subjects.　But in the case of imbasing coine, the proposition of gaine is fallacious, aiming only at a transient profit to the prince alone, which is sure to be followed with a manifold and lasting disprofit, both to the prince and people, for the reasons hereafter expressed.[a]

1. First; touching the point of profit, mony being the necessary of *Profit 1.* all things,—If brasse mony be coined and made currant, his Majestie

---

[a] Rushworth, pt. ii. vol. ii. p. 1217-19, gives Sir Thomas Rowe's speech against the coining of brass money, but no other; the following seems to be the digest of the arguments on both sides rather than the speech of any particular individual.

will loose such proportion, in all his revenues and customes, as the same shall differ from the present standerd, and every private man will loose in his rentes and estates accordingly.

2. The trade of the kingdome, as touching foreine partes, will be at a stand, or much disturbed; for that, when the rule is uncertaine, merchants will not be encouraged to send their commodities to a doubtfull market, which will consequently hinder his Majesties customes.

3. The commerce at home will likewise be disordered, for that those which have monies in bancke will be afraid to lend or employ. Then those that have mony abroad will call it in, and either keepe them in theire hands, or remit them into other partes, while the exchange is high. The very rumor of an intent to coine brasse mony having laid the ground of some prejudice already.

4. All lenders of mony will in particuler manner be damnified; and if, to prevent the same, they shold but suddenly call in theire mony, it may not only disaccommodate, but occasion the hurte and detriment of many his Majesties subjects, who, to drive their trade, must of necessity take up mony at high rate, when there is scarcity, which they now have at easie rates; which will by consequence occasion, in shorte time, a great slacking of trade, and diminution of his Majesties customes.

5. The exchanges are now for Antwerpe at 36s. 8d.; for Hamburge at 36s. 3d.; for Amsterdam at 37s. 3d.; for Roterdam at 37s. 6d : but, if brassemony shall have a currencie, the exchanges will presently fall, by necessary consequence, and will occasion the transportation of gould and silver out of his Majesties kingdome.

6. It will abate the value of our clothe and other native commodities, and raise the value of fforeine commodities, because our being bought cheaper here will be sould cheaper there, and they will demande more for theires, because our mony is so much courser.

7. Howsoever our mony shall be raised or let fall, the proceedings of trade will be grounded upon the intrinsecall and true value, and

not upon the denomination thereof. Leather mony, in the time of king Edward I., and copper mony since then, not having beene more valued abroad then the metalles were worth; nor at home, but of promise of repayment of so much as they are currant at.

8. It will finally inriche him only who hath the mines of silver; viz. the king of Spaine; for that though other nations may serve themselves, and after a time make advantage of our inhansing the price of monies, yet it will redound to his selfebenefit, the ende being the firste owner and propriator thereof, the embasing of our coine driving the same effect which the inhansing will doe.

9. The Scottes cannot desire a greater advantage then this, for that, by imitation and following this course, they will make 50 li. goe as farre as 200 li. nowe.

10. By this way, the course of exchange will be stopped, as it hath relation to this kingdome, in regard that merchants and bankers in all countries, in delivery of their monies, have consideration only of the true value, and not of the promising currancie thereof: and if no exchange, no commerce can be.

11. The coining of brassemony will availe his Majesties service at most but once, and can never produce so advantageous an effect as to recompense the damage to his Majestie, and inconveniences to his subjects, which it will for ever after produce.

If any greate inconvenience shall appeere by these brassemonies, Objection 1. the King, upon giving satisfaction, may decry them when he pleaseth.

By this his Majestie and his subjects will not only be loosers, but Answer. all Foreiners will be gainers; because, when any discompts have been evened, according to the rate as monies have been altered, whoso- ever abroad shall by his trade have any estate in England, shall gaine thereby, and some of his Majesties subjects may be double loosers. And moreover, it is to be feared that, besides what shall be coined by his Majesties order here in England, such further quantity may be either counterfeited here, or imported from the partes beyond the seas, as may render it almost impossible to be remedied, without the

infinite losse of his Majestie, or ruine to his subjects.    Witnesse th
blacke mony in Spaine.

Objection 2.      Other nations have altered theire coines; why shold not hi
Majestie doe the same?

Answer.      No other nations have altered theire coine but to their grea
damage; for, since the last change upon the coines in France, the
crowne, which was before worth 6*s.* sterling, by way of exchange, ii
now worth but 4*s.* 3*d.*, or thereabout; which is about 40 per centun
that the French mony is undervalued, besides the great prejudice
they have susteined in theire trade.    The like and worse events have
been in Germany and elsewhere.    Finis.

September 14.    Reported that the Scottes have seated themselves
at Newcastle, and have fortified it seven miles in compasse; that they
have Tinmouth Castle, well furnished with ordonance, &c.    That the
King's writtes are out to all the lords spirituall and temporall, to be
at Yorke 24 of this month, to advise for the safety of the kingdome.

Parliament.      November 3.    A parliament began: God grant a blessing!

The newes is that the Queene-mother [a] goeth away.

The Lord Deputie of Ireland [b] is questioned.

Sir Thomas Beecher, for serching the pockets of the earl of Warwicke, lord Say, and lord Brookes, so soone as the last parliament
was broken up.

Monopolies goe downe.

Secretary Windebanke questioned for licenses to Jesuites.    Sir
Henry Speller for Papists.

November 17 (Queen Elisabeth's day) a fast at London.    De-

Fast.      cember 8 in the country.    At St. Margaret's, Westminster, (the
House of Commons there,) the second service was beaten out by a
psalme sung, whether by accident or of purpose, qu? In the chappel

Bishop of Lin-      the Bishop of Lincolne [c] read prayers before the upper house; he is
coln.      restored, and was the next day in his robes in the parliament house.

---

[a] Mary de Medicis, then visiting England.

[b] The Earl of Strafford.

[c] Dr. Williams, formerly Lord Keeper.

Mr. Prin[a] sent for.   His man (as some called him), his servant, or Mr. Prin.
frend, or deere well-willer, who was long since whipped and imprisoned, is released.   Mr. Burton [b] and Dr. Bastwicke[c] sent for:
Dr. Laiton too.[d]

Many railes[e] were pulled downe, before the parliament; at Ippis-
wich, Sudbury, &c. Marlowe, Bucks: the organs too, &c.

Doctor Chaderton,[f] once master of Emmanuel, died, and was Dr. Chaderton.
buried at Cambridge, November 16.

In Paules church lately, a great tumult against doctor Ducke
and others in the high commission within the consistory; who
escaping, much outrage was shewed in the consistorie to the seates,
&c.   The Bishops, guarded with musket-men, came to the convoca-
tion-house.   *Plura si Deus velit.*

November 3, 1640.   His Majesties gracious Speech conteined
in it these two maine pointes: that he committed to the parliament the busines of the Scottish rebelles, and the redresse of their
greevances; yet withall he advertised of the mony taken up of the
city of London by lords who had engaged themselves for repayment;
and that, whereas the Scottish army was to be provided for, for two
monthes, he was lothe that for want of monies his owne army shold
be disbanded before that time.

It is said, that the Lord Keeper, in his speech, affirmed that the
lords had assented to a warre with the Scottes; but it is also said
that a charge is given to amend the copies of the speech thus:
" Some of the lords have assented to a warre with the Scottes."[g]

---

[a] See Rushworth, pt. iii. vol. i. pp. 20, 67, 74, 228.

[b] Ibid. pp. 20, 67, 78, 207, 213.          [c] Ibid. pp. 20, 79, 80, 119, 193, 203, 283.

[f] Laurence Chaderton, B.D. the first Master of Emmanuel college, resigned that office
in 1622.   When he died, he was, it is said, in the 103rd year of his age.   It would seem
he was buried in the old chapel of Emmanuel college.   Cleveland has an elegy on Dr.
Chaderton, occasioned by his long-deferred funeral.—Cooper, Annals of Cambridge,
iii. 305.

[d] Ibid. pp. 20, 228, 229.                       [e] *i. e.* altar-rails.

[g] The Speech is printed without this modification in Rushworth, pt. iii. vol. i. pp. 13-16.

MY LORDS,

I doe expect that you will hastily make a perfect relation unto the house ᵇ of these great affaires for which I have called you hether, and of the trust and repose ᶜ in them, and how freely I have put my selfe upon theire loves and affections at this time.  And that you may knowe the better how to doe so, I shall explane my selfe concerning one thing I spake the last day.  I told you the rebelles were to be put out of this kingdome.  It is true I must needes call them so, so long as they have an army that doth invade us; yet I am now under a treatie with them, and under my greate seale I call them subjects, and so they are too.  But the estate of the affaires is shortly this.  It is true I did expect, when I did call the lords and greate ones to Yorke, to have mette you at this time only, to have given you a gracious answer to all your greevances, for I was in good hope, by theire wisedomes and assistance, to have made an end of that busines; but I must tell you that my subjects of Scotland did so delay them, that it was not possible for me to end that there.  I can in no wise blame the lords that mett at Rippon that the treatie was not ended, but must thanke them for theire industry and paines ; and certainly, had they had as much power as affection, I shold by this time have made an ende.

But now the treaty is transferred from Rippon to London, where I shall conclude nothing without your knowledge, and I doubt not but with your approbation, for that I doe not desire to have these great workes done in a corner.  I shall hereafter open all the steppes of this misunderstanding, and cause of these great differences betwixt me and my subjects of Scotland ; and I doubt not but with your assistance I shall make them knowe theire duties, and by your assistance make them returne whether they will or no.

FINIS.

The erle of Bristow or lord Digby, being with the King the last yeere, 1639, was (*ut dicitur*) charged to speake his mind about the Scottish warres; and, though unwilling, made this answer, " I attend your Majestie here, tendring my service with my best care to see your Majestie safe; for if you miscarrie, I, and all that assent to this warre, without the consent of the body of the realme, shall

ᵃ Printed less perfectly in Rushworth, pt. ii. vol. ii. p. 1336.
ᵇ " House of Commons."   R.                    ᶜ " I have reposed."   R.

utterly perish, if there be a parliament." A doctor at Paul's ser November 18.
mon told me this. It was currant in many men's mouthes that
the lord chamberlane[a] (and another lord in like sorte) told the
King, that if he gave backe and altered his resolution about this
parliament, that he and his were lost, and willed the King to
looke well how safe he and his should stand.

Judge Reeve,[b] this summer assises, did in Southwarke refuse to
proceede upon the inditement of one of the Lambeth tumult (before mentioned), saying that he wold have no hand in any man's
bloud; but, because the fellow had been busie, &c. remitted him
to prison againe. Sir William Beecher was committed to the usher
of the blacke rod for not disclosing his warrant to serche the pockets
of erle of Warwicke, lord Say, lord Brooke, presently after the last
parliament broken up. It was done the next morne to the lord
Say and lord Brooke in bedde; the lord Brooke's lady being in Ut prius.
bed with him [c] (*ut dicitur*). The King at length affirming that he
commanded it, he was released.

Spain in an uprore, or discontent between themselves. Portugal ij revolted.

A DIALOGUE BETWEEN TWO ZELOTS, CONCERNING " ETC." IN THE NEWE OATH.[d]

> St. Roger,[e] from a zealous piece of freeze,
> Rais'd to a vicar, but without degrees;[f]
> Whose yeerly auditt may, by strict accompt,
> To xx nobles and his veiles amount;

---

[a] Philip Earl of Pembroke and Montgomery.

[b] Sir Edward Reeve, justice of the common pleas. See Smyth's Obituary, p. 23.

[c] Rushworth, pt. ii. vol. ii. p. 1167, mentions that his study was searched, but nothing
further. A contemporaneous record of events in Sloane MS. 1467, f. 104, mentions a
personal search, and says that " Lord Brookes had taken from him a discourse between
Mr. Cotton, a minister now in New England, and Mr. Ball, concerning our church liturgy,
one being to mainteine it against the other's opposing it. Hee had alsoe some peticions to
complaine of some greivances, one being from silent ministers to desire there might not be
soe heavy a hand carried over them."

[d] Collated with a contemporaneous copy in Sloane MS. 1467, chap. i. There is
another copy in Addit. MS. 6396, fol. 15.          [e] " Sir Roger."

[f] " Of the children's threes."

Fedde on the common of the female charity,
Untill the Scottes can bring about theire parity,—
So shotten that his soule, much like himselfe,
Walkes but in quirpo ; this same clergie elfe,
Encountring with a brother of the cloath,
Fell presently to cudgels with the Oath.
The quarrell was a strange mis-shapen monster,
*Et cætera* (God blesse us) which they conster,—
The brand upon the buttocke of the beast,
The dragon's tayle tied on a knott,—a neast
Of yong apocryphas, the fashion
Of a new mentall reservation.
Whiles Roger thus derides [a] the text, the other
Winkes and expoundes, saying, " My pious brother
Hearken with reverence, for the point is nice ;
I never read on 't but I fasted twice,
And so by revelation know it better
Then all the learnde idolaters of the letter."
With that he swelde, and sette upon the theame
Like great Goliah with his weaver's beame :
" I say to the,[b] *Et Cætera*, thou lyest,
Thou art the curled locke of Anti-Christ ;
Rubbish of Babel, for who will not say,
Tongues are confounded in *et cætera ?*
Who sweares *et cætera* sweares more oathes at once,
Then Cerberus out of his triple sconce ;
Who viewes it well, with the same eye beholdes
The ould false serpent in his numerous foldes ;
Accurs'd *et cætera*, now, now I sent,
What the prodigious bloudy oysters meant.
Oh Bowker, Bowker,[c] how camst thou to lacke
This fiend, in thy prophetick almanacke ?
'Tis the darke vault where the infernall plott
Of powder 'gainst the state was first begotte ;
Peruse the Oath, and you shall soon descry it,
By all the Father Garnets that stand by it ;
'Gainst which the Church, whereof I am a member
Shall keep another fifth day of November.

[a] " divides."          [b] "thee."          [c] " Booker."

Nay, heeres not all; I cannot halfe untrusse
*Et cœtera*, it is so abdominous.
The Trojan nagge was not so fully lin'de,
Unrippe *et cœtera*, and you shall finde
Ogg, the great commissary, and, which is worse,
The apparitor upon the skew-balde horse.
Then, finally, my babe of grace, forbeare;
Et cætera will be too large to sweare,
For 'tis (to speake in a familiar style)
A Yorkshire way-bit, longer then a mile."
Heere Roger was inspirde, and by God's diggers,
Hee'le sweare in wordes at length and not in figures;
No; by this drinke which he takes of, as loath
To leave *et cœtera* in his liquid oath;
His brother pledgde him, and in that bloudy wine
He sweares hee'l be the synod's Cataline.
Thus they dranke on, not offering to parte,
Till they had sworne out the eleventh quart;
Whiles all that heard and saw them jointly say,
They and theire tribe were all—*et cœtera*.

In cathedra derisorum ne sedeam.   Psalm i.

Upon Tuisday, November 17, when the fast was kept at London for the parliament, &c., I was at St. Paul's church, where one Mr. Stanwicke (or Kanwicke), a chaplein to my lord of Ely, preached on Nehemiah, i. verse 4, who upon just occasion, in opening the story of the Jewish pressures and calamities which caused Nehemiah to fast, &c., did say that the care of the Jewes to have Jerusalem rebuilded in her walles, and the gates set up, was not to mainteine rebellion and keepe out the King's authority, but to defend themselves against Tobiah, Sanballah, and such great men as under the King (whom they flattered with lies) sought to oppresse them.

Out of the last wordes of the first booke of Polychron. fol. 70, this is taken.[a]   " But among all Englishmen medled together is so great changing and diversity of clothing and aray, and so many maner and diversity of shapes, that well nigh is there any man

Polychronic. prophecie.

[a] Edit. 1482, printed by Caxton.

knowne by his clothing and his aray of whatsoever degree that he
be; thereof prophesied an holy anker in king Egelfred's time in this
manner:—Henricus, lib. 6°. 'Englishmen, forasmuch as they use
them to dronkelewnes, to treason, and to rychlesnes of God's hows,
first by Danes and then by Normans, and at thirde time by Scottes,
that they holde most wretched and lest worth of all other, they
shall be overcome.  Then the world shall be so unstable, and so
diverse and variable, that the unstablenes of thoughts shall be bito-
kened by many manner diversities of clothing.  *Explicit liber
primus."* [a]

*Anachorite.* (margin note)

BY THE KING.

A PROCLAMATION FOR A GENERALL FAST, TO BE KEPT THROUGHOUT THE REALME<br>OF ENGLAND.[b]

The newes is that secretary Windbanke, and Reade his secretary
were fledde, ere the house knewe it.

That the shipmony was voted, without gainsaying, to be against
lawe.

That sixteen of the house were sent to eight judges, to knowe who
pressed or persuaded in the busines of shipmony.

That there is an order for a transcript into the country, that
recusants must all be endicted the next sessions, December 9.

THE LORD OF STRAFFORD'S ACCUSATION.

[Omitted, being in print.]

THE LORD FALKLAND HIS SPEECH IN PARLIAMENT.[c]

Mr. Speaker,

*Lord Deputie.* (margin note)

I rejoice very much to see this day, and the want hath line not in mine

*About the judg-
ment late given
for Shipmony.* (margin note)

---

[a] See Scriptores post Bedam, Henry Huntingdon's Hist. p. 309, end of book i. and
p. 359, beginning of book vi.

[b] Printed in Fœdera, vol. ix. pt. iii. p. 34.  Sir Benjamin Ruddierd's and Sir Robert
Dering's speeches follow; but both are omitted as being in print.

[c] Rushworth, pt. ii. vol. ii. pp. 1342, 1351, gives parts of a speech of lord Falkland in
this parliament, but it differs entirely from the present.

affections, but my lungs, if to all that hath beene past my voice hath not been as loud as any man's in the house; yet truly mine opinion is, we have yet done nothing if we doe not more.    I shall adde what I humbly conceive ought to be added, as soone as I have said something with reference to him that saies it.

I will first desire the forgivenes of the House if in ought I say I seeme to intrenche upon another's profession, and enter upon the worke of another robe; since I have been entrusted by the report of another committee, and confirmed by the uncontradicted rule of the whole house; since I shall say nothing in this kind, but in order to somewhat further, and which moves me to venture mine opinion and to expect your pardon ; since I am confident that history alone is able to shewe this judgment contrary to our lawes, and logicke alone sufficient to prove it distractive to our proprieties, which every free and noble person values more then his possession.    I will not professe what I knowe of my selfe, and all those who knowe me knowe it of me, that my naturall disposition is farre from inclyning to severity, much less to cruelty; that I have no particular provocations from their persons, and have particular obligations to theire callings, against whom I am to speake ; *and that, though not for much, yet for more then I have;* for I hope it will be beleeved that only publike interest hath extorted this from me ; and that which I would not say, if I conceived is not both so true and so necessarie that no undigested meate can be heavier upon the stomacke then this unsaid wolde have layne upon my conscience.

* Mr. Speaker,[a] the constitution of this Commonwelth hath established, or rather endeavoured to establish, to us the security of our goods, and the security of those lawes which should secure us our goods, by appointing for us judges so setled, so sworne, that there can be no oppression, but they of necessity must be accessary.    Since, if they neither denie nor delay us justice, (which neither for the greate nor the litle seale they ought to doe), the greatest person in the kingdome cannot continue the least violence upon the meanest. But the [b] security, Mr. Speaker, hath beene almost our ruine ; this bulwarke for us hath been turned, or rather turned it selfe, into a battery against us ; and those persons which shold have been as dogges to defend the flocke have been the wolfe to worrie it.

* These judges, Mr. Speaker, to instance not them only, but theire greatest crime, have delivered an opinion and a judgment, the first in an extrajudiciall manner, and both in an extrajudiciall matter, that is such as came not within

---

a This and those of the subsequent paragraphs to which an asterisk is prefixed, are printed in Rushworth, pt. ii. vol. ii. App. p. 242.

b " this," Rushworth.

theire cognisance, they being judges, and neither philosophers nor polititians. In which, when it is so absolute and evident, the lawe of the lande, and that of generall reason and equity (by which particuler lawes at first were framed), returnes to her throne and government, where *salus populi* becomes not only *suprema* but *sola lex*. At which and to which ende, whosoever a wold dispence with the King to make use of our mony dispences with us to make use of his and one another's. In the judgment, they contradicted both many and cleere acts and declarations of parliaments, and those in this very case, and in this very reigne; so that for them they needed to have consulted with no other recordes but theire memories.

\* Secondly, they have contradicted apparant evidences, by supposing weightie and evident b dangers, in the most serene, quiet, and halcyon daies that could possibly be imagined, a fewe contemptible pirats being our most formidable enemies, and there being neither prince nor state with and from whom we have not either embassadors or amity or both.

\* Thirdly, they contradicted the writte it selfe, by supposing that supposed danger to be so suddaine that it could not stay for a parliament, which required but forty dayes stay; the writte being in no such hast, but being content to stay seven monthes, which is that time four times over.

\* Mr. Speaker, it seemed generallie strange that they who sawe not the lawes, which all men else sawe, should see that danger which no man saw but themselves; yet, though this begate the more generall wonder, three other particulers begate the more generall indignation.

The first, if all the reasons for this judgment were such that they needed not any from the adverse parte to helpe them to convert those fewe who had before the least suspition of the legality of that most illegall writte, there being fewer that approved of the judgment then there were that judged it, for I am confident they did not that themselves.

\* Secondly, when they had allowed to the King the sole power in necessity, the sole judgment of necessity, and by that enabled him to take both from us what he wold, when he wold, and of whom c he wolde, they yet contented d us enough to offer to persuade us that they had left us our properties. The third and last is, and which I confesse moved me most, that by the transformation of this e from the state of free subjects (a good phrase, Mr. Speaker, under Mr.

---

a "whatsoever," margin.          b "eminent," Rushworth.

c "how he would," margin and Rushworth.

d "contemned," margin; the latter is the true reading.

e "us," Rushworth.

Heylin's favour) into that of villaines, they disabled us, by legall and voluntary supplies, to expresse our affections to his Majestie, and by that to cherish
his to us (that is, to parliaments).    Mr. Speaker, the cause of all miseries we
have suffered, and the cause of all the jealousies that we have had that we shold
yet suffer more, is that a most excellent prince hath been most infinitely abused,
his judges telling him that in lawe, his divines telling him that in conscience,
his counsellors telling him that in policy, he might doe what he pleased.

With the first of these we are nowe to deale, which may be a good leading
case to the rest; and since, in the penning of these lawes, upon which these men
have trampled, our ancestors have shewed their utmost care and wisedome for
our uneffected security, wordes having done nothing, and yet done all that
words can doe, we must nowe be forced to thinke of abolishing our greevances,
by abolishing our greevers; of taking away this judgment and these judges
together, and of regulating theire successors by theire most exemplary punishment who wold not regulate themselves by most evident lawes.    Of the degrees
of this punishment I will not speake.    I will only say we have accused a greate
person of high treason, for intending to subvert our fundamentall lawes, and
introduce an arbitrary government; whereas what we suppose he meant to doe
we are sure they have done, there being no lawe more fundamentall then that
they have alreadie subverted, and no government more absolute then that they
have really introduced.    Mr. Speaker, not only the severe punishment, but the
suddaine removeall of these men will have a very large effect, in one very considerable consideration.    We only accuse, and the House of the Lords condemnes,
in which condemnation they usually receive advice, though not direction, from
the judges; and I leave it to every man to imagine how prejudiciall to us, that
is to the Commonwealth, and how partiall to theire fellowe malefactors the
advice of such judges is like to be; how undoubtedlie, for theire owne sakes,
they will conduce theire power, that every action be judged to be a lesse faulte,
and every person to be lesse faulty, then in justice they ought to be.

Amongst these, Mr. Speaker, there is one I must not loose in the croude,
whom I doubt not but we shall finde, when we examine the reste of them, with
what hopes they have been tempted, by what feares they have been assailed,
and by whose importunity they have been pursued, before they consented to
what they did : I doubt not, I say, but we shall then finde him to have been a
most admirable solliciter, but a most abhominable judge.

He it is who not only gave away with his breath what our ancestors had
purchased for us, by so large an expence of theire time, theire care, theire
treasure, and theire bloud, and imploied an industry as greate as his injustice,
to persuade others to joine with him in that deed of gifte, but strove to roote
up those liberties which they had cutte downe, and to make our greevances

immortall, and our slavery irreparable, least any parte of our posterity might want occasion to curse him, when he declared that power to be so inherent to the crowne, as that it was not in the power even of a parliament to divide them.

I have heard, Mr. Speaker (and I thinke heere), that common fame is enough for this house to accuse upon, and then undoubtedly enough to be accused upon in this house. She hath reported this so generally, that I expect not that you shold bid me name him whom you all knowe, nor doe I looke to telle you newes, when I tell you tis the [a] Lord Keeper ; [b] but this I thinke fitte to put you in mind, that his place admittes him to his Majestie's eare, and trustes him with his Majestie's conscience ; and how prejudicious every moment must be to us, whilst the one gives him meanes to infuse such unjust opinions of this house into his Majestie as are expreste in that libell rather then Declaration, of which many beleeves him to have been the principall secretary ; and the other puttes the vast and almost unlimited power of the Chancery into such handes, which in the safest wold be dangerous : for my parte, I thinke no man here secure that he shall thinke himselfe worth any thing when he rises, whilest all our estates are in his brest who hath sacrificed his country to his ambition ; whilst he who hath prostituted his owne conscience hath the keeping of the King's, and he who hath undone us alreadie by wholesale hath a power left in him of undoing us by retaile.

Mr. Speaker, in the beginning of this parliament, he told us, and I am confident every man here beleeved it before he told it, and not the more for his telling of it, though a sory witnes is a good testimony against himselfe, that his Majestie never required any thing from any of his ministers but justice and integrity ; against which, if any of them had transgressed, upon their heades, and that deservedly, it was to fall. And truly, after he hath in this saying pronounced his owne condemnation, we shall be more partiall to him then he is to himselfe if we be slowe to pursue it.

It is therefore my just and humble motion that we may choose a select committee, to drawe up his and theire charges, and to examine their cariage of this particuler, to make the use of it in the charge, and if he shall be found guilty of tampering with judges against the publike security, who thought tampering with witnesses in a private case worthy of so severe a fine, if he shall be found to have gone beyond the rest to this [c] judgment, and to have gone beyond the rest in this judgment, that in the punishment for it, the justice of this house may not denie him the due honor both to precede and exceed the rest.

---

[a] " my," in margin.

[b] Sir John Finch.   See his impeachment in Harl. Miscell. vol. v. p. 566.

[c] "that," margin.

I hate these following railing rimes,
Yet keepe them for president of the times.

### A DISMALL SUMMONS TO THE DOCTORS' COMMONS.

Thou cage full of fowle birds and beasts,
　　Attend this dismall doome .;
The canonites now murthered are,
　　With canons of theire owne.
Civilians civill villanes are,
　　Ould doting knaves are Doctors ;
Notorious knaves are notaries,
　　Bold prating knaves are proctors.
The registers regrators are,
　　Thy summoners scumme of creatures,
Thy delegates and advocates
　　Are cosening knaves and cheators.
Thy chancelors and officials
　　Match Machiavel in evill ;
They make God's house a denne of theeves,
　　And keepe courte for the Devill.
Thy court is called Christian,
　　Yet Anti-Christian is ;
The court of hell is not so fell
　　And devilish as is this.
Thy bishops they are bite-sheepes,
　　Thy deanes they nowe are dunces,
Thy priestes they are the priests of Baal;
　　The Devill take all in bunches !

---

U R I C [a], pore Canterburie, in a tottering state,
P O P E [b] some say youde be, but now t's too late.
R U 2 YY [c] for all those eyes are now upon you ?
U R A K [d] if that you say that they will wrong you.
S C O T some say was he brought all to light,
I C U R [e] in a greate feare your lawne's not white,
A Grig R Y [f] if he comes nigh, he'le have the miter,
H E A D and all for me hee'l fall the lighter.

---

[a] You are, I see.
[b] A copy in Sloane MS. 1489 reads, " A P O P they say you'll be, but tis to late."
[c] Are you too wise.　　　　[d] You are a K.　　　　　　　[e] I see you are.
[f] A Gregory.

[GOD HAVE MERCY, GOOD SCOT.]

[a] You crafty projectors, why hang you your head ?
Promoted, informed,[b] what are you all dead ?
Or will you beyond sea to frolike and playe
With Sir Giles Montpeston,[c] who led you the way ?
    If Simson and Dudly [d] have left you the lotte,
    A twist readie spun, God have mercy, good Scott.

How high were they [e] flowne in their [e] flying hope,
Theire [e] patents for pinnes, tobacco, and soape,
They yeerely received for enhancing of wine,
False dice and false cardes, besides the great fine.
    The tide is now turned, lets drinke th' other pot,
    And merily sing, God have mercy, good Scott.

Shall one man alone all trading ingrosse ?
And build up his fortune by other men's losse ?
That he may jette it [f] in dauncing and whoring,
For which the subject is ever more soring,[g]
    The title and honour these gallants have got,
    May fall in the fier, God have mercy, good Scott.

To play at boh peepe our Catholikes strive,
Who lately with the Devill a bargaine did drive,
The peace of this kingdome for ever to marre,
To change our late plenty to famine and warre :
    But now 'tis believed theyle pay the whole shott
    When th' reckoning doth come, God a' mercy, good Scott.

What is there no helpe at such a deade lifte ?
To put of the parliament is there no shifte ?
Nor dare they repose any faith in theire creed ?
Will not Ave Maries helpe them at their need ?
    The House is acquainted with every plott ;
    Theire [h] mines are blowne up, God a' mercy, good Scott.

---

[a] Collated with a copy in Harl. MS. 4931, f. 80, where the burden is " Gramercy, good Scott."        [b] " Promoters, informers."

[c] " Mompesson," margin.  He was a notorious delinquent in the matter of alehouse licenses, in the reign of James the First, and fled the country to avoid the rigour of the law. See the Progresses, &c. of James I. vol. iii. pp. 660, 666.

[d] " Epson," Harl. MS.   Empson and Dudley, the extortioning ministers of Henry VII.
[e] " You " and " your."    [f] " And he for to sette it."    [g] " goring."
[h] " You " and " your " throughout.

Where be our proud prelates that straddle so wide,
As if they did meane the worlde [a] to bestride,
To tread on the nobles, to trample them downe,
To set up the mitre above the King's crowne,
    That ere he was clerke the priest hath forgot;
    But pride will come downe, God a' mercy, good Scott.

With scriptures divines doe play [d] fast and loose,
And turne holy writ to capon and goose;
Theire gutt is theire God, religion they mocke,
To pamper theire flesh they famish theire flocke,
    To preach and to pray they have all [c] forgott,
    But now they'le be taught, God a' mercy, good Scott.

Although that this iland abound in all crimes,
The Parliament sayes we shall have good times,
Then let us not faint as things without hope,—
An halter for traytors, a fig for the Pope!
    Let Spaine and the Strumpet of Babilon plott,
    Yet we shall be safe, God a' mercy, good Scott.

The Miter shall be given away [d] to the poore,
The city shall cozen the country no more ;
Oppression shall downe, then justice shall smile,
French and Popery shall be banishte this ile.[e]
    Religion shall florish without any blotte,[f]
    When this comes to passe, God a' mercy, good Scott.

An order made to a select committee chosen by the whole House of Commons to receive Petitions touching ministers.

London, printed by J. D. for Henry Overton, and are to be sold at his shop entring into Pope's head alley out of Lumbard streete, 1640.

THE NAMES OF THE COMMITTEES CHOSEN DECEMBER 19, 1640.

Alderman Pennington.

Sir Thomas Hutchinson, &c. to the number of 62, whereof two were Rowse's, gent.

---

[a] " The moone."        [b] " With Scripture divine they."        [c] " almost."
[d] " The miser shall give all away."
[e] " French toies and popery wee'le banish the ile."        [f] " plott."

This committee is to take into theire consideration the petition of the inhabitants of Huyendam[a] in the county of Buckingham, and all other petitioners of that nature; and also to consider how there may be preaching ministers set up where there are none, and how those preaching ministers may be mainteined where there is no maintenance, and when they are in, how they may be kept and mainteined; and to receive all other petitions of the like nature.    And it is further ordered that the committee shall have power to send for parties, witnesses, writings, and recordes, that may conduce to the busines in question, before them.    This was a sub-committee made by the grand committee for religion; and it is this day ordered that this committee shall from the House have the like power it formerly had, and consider and enquire of the true ground and causes of the great scarcity of preaching ministers throughout the whole kingdome; and to consider of some way for removing of scandalous ministers, and putting others in theire places.    And it is further ordered that all the knights and burgesses for every county be required from this House, both upon theire owne knowledge and upon information from the severall counties where they dwell, within six weekes, to informe this house of the state and conditions of their counties concerning preaching ministers, and whence it ariseth there is such a scarcity of them thoroughout the kingdome.    It is earnestly desired and expected by the Parliament that all ingenuous persons in every county of this kingdome will be very active to improve the present opportunity by giving a true information of all the parishes in theire severall counties—

1. Where there are men of more then one benefice, and what such men's revenues are reputed to be.

2. Where there is no maintenance or too litle maintenance for a preaching minister.

3. Where there is no preaching or seldome preaching.

---

[a] " Hugenden " in Journals of the House of Commons, ii. 54.

4. Where there are persecuting, innovating, or scandalous ministers, that they may be put out, and order taken for better to be put in theire places.

A Committee is chosen purposely to receive petitions and informations of this nature, and to take speciall care about so weighty a business. The Committee desires informations from all parties, if it be possible, within this monthe, as appeereth by the order given out by the Parliament, the 19th of this instant December, 1640.

The newes is certaine for Portugall revolted. It is said that the silver fleet, being endangered by the Hollanders, put into Portugall harbors, and is there stayed. The newes is that the Swedes have begirte the emperor and electors, at a diet in Germany. *Portugall.*

Newes of the Prince of Condie and others, up in armes in France.

Newes of Naples revolting from Spaine.

A matche between Lady Mary and the Prince of Orange's eldest sonne.

About 10 or 11 of February, his Majestie, in the Upper house, made a speech: He signified to the lords that there had been a treatie entertained, and was like to continue; of this he acquaintes them, affirming that three things swayed with him: 1. The Hollanders a people fitte for us to retaine amitie with, &c. 2. There will be no disparagement for religion. 3. Theire assistance may much helpe to the reliefe of his sister and her issue. *A matche with Prince of Orange.*

12. At the terme's end, judge Bartlet led away by usher of blacke rod.[a]

13. A treason discovered (*ut dicitur*).

Other newes from our Parliament. The cannons, ship-mony, Scottish busines, Mr. Waller's speech, &c. see my great booke ✠ pag. 82.

[a] Sir Robert Berkeley, one of the justices of the King's bench; he was seized when on his judicial bench and taken to prison. He was one of the judges who gave opinion in favour of the King's levying ship-money; was impeached in 1637, but escaped conviction till the impeachment was renewed in 1640. See Rushworth, pt. ii. vol. i. p. 606; pt. iii. vol. i. pp. 318-9. Clarendon, Hist. Rebell. vol. ii. p. 499.

THE HEADS OF THE SCOTTES LAST ARTICLES CONCERNING A DURABLE PEACE.
MARCH, 1640.

1. They desire unity in religion and conformity in church goverment.

2. That some of the Scottish men of eminency may attend the King and Prince.

3. That none be about his Majestie and Prince but those of the reformed religion.

4. Concerning the manner of chusing the councell and men in office in Scotland.

5. For naturalizing and mutuall priviledges of both nations.

6. Concerning customes in both kingdomes, both foreine and domesticke.

7. Freedome of trade.

8. Concerning manufactures and mutuall association of trade, both by sea and land.

9. Concerning the allay of coine and the liberty of free fishing for both nations.

10. An act of oblivion of by-gone deedes to be forgotten of both kingdomes.

11. An act for ratifying this present treatie and articles.

12. No invasion against either kingdome without an Act of Parliament.

13. If any hostility be offered by sea or land by any of either nation, that they be punished as enemies to State.

14. That neither of the two nations shall engage themselves in warre without consent of both nations.

15. Mutuall assistance against all forreine invasions.

16. Concerning removing of offenders in either of the kingdomes.

17. Concerning executing of decrees and sentences in both kingdomes, not having the originals but copies.

18. About the borders and middle-marches.

19. That the peace to be nowe established be inviolablie observed in all time to come.

20. All offenders to be punished in the trienniall parliaments of both nations. And that commissioners may be appointed of both kingdomes, for the conserving of peace in the intervall between parliaments.

THE SCHOLLER'S COMPLAINT, TO THE TUNE OF ALLOO, ALLOO, FOLLOW MY FANCY.

> All in a mellanchollike study,
>   None but my selfe,
> Me thought my muse grew muddy,
>   After seaven yeeres reading
>   And costly breeding,
> I fell and could finde no pelfe.
>   Into learned ragges I've read my plush and satten,
>   And now am fitte to begge in Greeke and Latine,
>   Instead of Aristotle I would I had a patten.[a]
>     Alas, pore scholler!
>     Whether wilt thou goe?
>
> Cambridge, I must leave thee,
>   And follow Fate;
> Colledge hopes deceive me,
>   Ofte I expected
>   To be elected,
> But desert is reprobate.
>   Masters of colledges have no common graces,
>   They that have fellowships have no common places,
>   And they that schollers are must have handsome faces.
>     Alas, pore scholler!
>     Whither wilt thou goe?
>
> I bowed, I have bended,
>   And all in hope,
> One day to be befrended;
>   I preach't, I printed,
>   What ere I hinted,
> To please our English pope.

[a] Qu. " patent "? in allusion to the monopolies so numerous during the early part of this reign.

I worshipt to the East that sunne doth now forsake me;
I finde I am falling, the Northerne windes doe shake me,
Would I'de beene upright, for bowing now doth breake me.
    Alas, pore scholler ! &c.

Into some country village
  Nowe I must goe,
Where neither tithe nor tillage
  The greedy patron
  And coached matron
Sweare to the Church they owe;
  But if I preach and pray too on the suddaine,
  And confute the Pope too, extempore without studying,
  I've tenne poundes a yeere, besides my Sunday pudding.
    Alas, pore scholler !
    Whether wilt thou goe ?

At greate preferment I aymed,
  Witnesse my silke;
But now my hopes are maymed.
  I lookt lately
  To have livde stately,
And a dayrie of bell ropes milke;
  But now, alas ! myselfe I must not flatter,
  Bigamy of steeples is an hanging matter,
  Each must have one, and curates will grow fatter.
    Alas, pore scholler !
    Whither wilt thou goe ?

The tongues and arts I've skill in,
  Divine and humane;
But all 's not worth a shilling.
  When the women heare me
  They will but jeere me,
And say I am profane.
  Once I remember I preached with a weaver;
  I quoted Austin,[a] he quoted Dod and Cleaver.[b]
  I nothing gotte, he got a cloake and beaver.
    Alas, pore scholler,
    Whither wilt thou goe ?

---

[a] St. Augustine.

[b] " Exposition of the Book of Proverbs, by John Dod, Robert Cleaver, and William Flinde."   4to. Lond. 1610-11.

Shippes, shippes, shippes I discover
 Crossing the maine;
Shall I in them saile over,
 Be jew or atheist,
 Turke or papist,
To Geneva or Amsterdam ?
 Bishoprickes are voide in Scotland; shall I thither ?
 Or shall I after Finch or Windebanke, to see if either
 Want a priest to shrive them ? oh no, 't is blustering weather.
  Alas, pore scholler !
  Whither wilt thou goe ?

Hoe, ho, ho ! I have hitt it ;
 Peace, Goodman foole,
Thou hast a trade will fitte it;
 Draw the indenture,
 Be bound at a venture
An apprentice to a free-schoole.
 Here thou art king, by William Lillies charter;
 Here thou maist whip and strip, hang, draw, and quarter,
 And committe to the redde rodde Tom, Jack, Will, and Arthur.
  I, I ! 'tis thither,
  Thither will I goe.

### [THE CANTERBURY BELL.]

Our Canterburie's greate cathedrall bell
Seldome ringes out but makes a fatall knell;
Her loud unpleasant jarring warring sound
The voice of all our sweet-tunde belles hath droun'd.
She lately rung so loud, without all doubt,
She strooke good Tom of Lincolne's clapper out.
It is reported by the men of Kent,
She sounds such discords, she gives no content ;
She ponderous is, she mightie great, the people
Would gladly plucke her quite out of the steeple;
She makes such hideous noise with her boom, boom,
As did the roaring bull which came from Rome;
But seeing that she 's made o' the Romish dresse,
She 'll serve the papists for to ring to masse.

### ON THE EARL OF STRAFFORD.

Here lies wise and valiant dust
Huddled up twixt fitte and just,

Strafford, who was hurried hence
Between treason and convenience,
Pass'd his time here in a miste.
Expound the riddle who so list,
His Prince's neerest joy and griefe,
Who had and wanted all reliefe,
The prop and ruine of the State,
The people's violent love and hate ;
One in extremes lovde and abhorde.
Riddles lie here ; or, in a worde,
Here lies bloud, and let it lie
Speechles still, and never crye.

THE MASSE-PRIEST'S LAMENTATION
FOR THE STRANGE ALTERATION
BEGUN IN THIS NATION,
WHEREFORE HE MAKES GREAT MONE,
AND SINGS O'HONE O'HONE,
TO THE TUNE OF POORE SHON.

St. Peter's seate
Is in a sweate,
    Alas ! alas !
The triple crowne
Is tumbled downe.
    Adew deere Masse !
Never shall I sippe
On Nunnes chery lippe ;
A halter or a whippe
    Is my doome,
Made of Scottish broome,
To sweepe us all to Rome.
    O hone, O hone !


Woe is me
This time to see,
    Alas ! alas !
A Puritan
The only man
    Will put downe Masse.

I fast, and I pray ;
My beades they take away,
And say I goe astray
    From the truth.
There's none will me relieve,
Therefore now may I grieve,
    O hone, O hone !

The Papists fine
With me did joine,
    Alas ! alas !
While there was hope
That the new Pope
    Would set up Masse.
But now he's downe
We all begin to frowne,
Which makes me in a swowne
    Thus to faint.
Oh helpe me some deere Saint,
And heare my sad complaint.
    O hone ! O hone !

Me Papist pore
Turnde out of dore,
　Alas! alas!
And holy Frier
Is in the mire.
　Farewell deere Masse!
For now all priests
Banished thou seest;
All pray to Christ,
　None to Mary,
To custome quite contrary;
That here him will not tary,
　O hone! O hone!

Some unknowne voyage,
Or pilgrimage,
　Alas! alas!
Through places strange
Now must I range,
　To find out Masse.
So till I come
Quite unto Rome,
Fortune at home
　Will not flatter,
Nor suffer holy water
Which we on browes did scatter.
　O hone! O hone!

The time is spent,
I shall be shent,
　Alas! alas!
If here I stay,
On beades to pray,
　And read more Masse.

If I recant,
Turne Protestant,
No pardon grant
　Will the Pope;
Then shall I want such hope,
If I religion coape,
　O hone! O hone!

Saint Marie's Creed
Be my good speed;
　Alas! alas!
Where should I run
This scourge to shun?
　Adew deere Masse.
Time with his whip
Makes me to skip,
Where should I slip
　Me to hide?
For such as Masse deride,
They cannot me abide,
　O hone! O hone!

Very sicke
Is Catholicke,
　Alas! alas!
The parliament
Is fully bent
　To put down Masse.
Jesuite and Frier
Hang in the bryer,
Like Dun in the mire,
　Well-a-day!
And those that were my stay
Must hang or runne away.
　O hone! O hone!
　　Is't not well, Sir?

### 7° APRILIS, 1642.

The lords and commons doe declare that they intend a due and necessary reformation of the government and leiturgie of the Church, and to take nothing away in the one or in the other, but what shall be evill or justly offensive, or at least unnecessary and burthensome.

And for the better effecting thereof, speedily to have consultation
with godly and learned divines: and, because this will never of itself
attein the end sought therein, they will therefore use their utmos
endevors to establish learned and preaching ministers, with a good
and sufficient maintenance throughout the whole kingdome, wherein
many darke corners are miserablie destitute of the meanes of salva
tion, and many poore ministers want necessary provision.[a]

VOTED BY BOTH HOUSES.

1. That the King shall not goe into Ireland.

2. That those that counselled the King to goe into Ireland are
enemies to the State and Kingdome.

3. Those that shall goe with the King to Ireland are traitors to
the King and State.

4. Those that shall lend the King any monies upon his parkes or
houses, shall loose theire monies, and be liable to the mercy of the
Parliament.

5. That what the Lords did in not going to the King when he
sent for them, was no more then is justifiable, in as much as the
publike did require it.

6. Those that shall take the places of the Lords are ignoble, and
unworthy to be members of the Common-wealth.

7. That no members of the House of Commons shall goe to the
King, without consent of the house.

There were, besides these, certaine reasons sent to his Majestie
shewing why they thus voted, &c.; as first, because his going into
Ireland wold be many wayes an hazard to his person, &c. See more
hereof.

The Parliament hath latelie taken the Militia of the kingdome into
theire power and disposing, about which there was some contestation;
and faine wold it have beene gotten that his Majestie might have had
the Militia of all the cities and corporations; or, if not so, yet that

1642, March.
April.

Militia.

---

[a] Printed with variations in Rushworth, pt. iii. vol. i. p. 560, under date of April 9th.

eche great town might have the disposing of its owne: but lately one Binion, a Silkeman of London, was censured for framing a <sup></sup>Binion cens. contra Petition, for London to have power of theire owne militia.<sup>a</sup> His censure was 3,000 p., a disabling to beare office in church or commonwealth, a losse of his Citie freedome and priviledges, and two yeeres' imprisonment in Colchester goale, if more were not afterwards imposed.<sup>b</sup>

April 25, Hockday.<sup>c</sup>   Newes that Aragon was revolted from Spain of certaine, as Portugall before.  That the French wold none of theire arbitrary government, but wold have a government like ours. Spain, Aragon, France.

That the King's atturney, Herbert, for drawing something about King's atturney, his Majestie's proceedings, was lately censured more then he was Herbert. worth, and for that he shewed himselfe crosse and stower, he was committed to the Fleet.

The many occurrences about the Parliament businesses, the Home newes. differences between the King's Majestie and them, theire Petitions, his answers (supposed or otherwise), the affairs of Ireland, &c. are extant in multitudes of bookes and papers (unto which God in mercy put an end!) but the newes of Suffolk in Bartholomewe weeke Insurrection at I here set downe briefly.  On Thursday August 25, late, at sunset Melford. or thereabout, came a warrant from sir William Castleton, high sheriffe, for all trained soldiers in our towne of Downham, (and so for others in that hundred,) with other able men, to appeere at Hargate heath by Bury, the next day, for suppressing of a rebellious company of about 2,000, &c.  They appeered, and refusing to goe with the sherife, or lay downe theire armes for others, at length Mr. North theire Captaine came, with whom they went, and on Friday apprehended some fewe of the company.  The lady Savage's house At Melford. was defaced; all glasse broken, all iron pulled out, all household stuffe gone, all sielings rent downe or spoiled, all likely places

<sup>a</sup> See Rushworth, pt. iii. vol. i. p. 779.      <sup>b</sup> See Clarendon, History, vol. i. p. 659.
<sup>c</sup> Hock-tide is a festival beginning the 15th day after Easter, which fell this year on April 10th.

CAMD. SOC.          R

digged where mony might be hidden, the gardens defaced, beere and
wine consumed, and let out (to knee deepe in the cellar), the
deere killed and chased out, &c.  The lady saith the losse is 40,000li
Sir Francis Mannocke's house [a] was pillaged of all goods; (and, as is
said, not his writings spared, which he craved, but were torne, nor
his dogs).  Also one Mr. Martin's house pillaged.  Doctor Warren's
house was rifled for his Gods, and a greate many set about the
market crosse, termed young ministers.  Him they huffed and
shuffed about, but (as is said) hurt not otherwise, though he say
they tooke mony from him.  This insurrection scareth all the
malignant party.  The Sunday following came letters signifying the

**Coventry busi-ness.** defeature at Coventry, where his Majestie *(as is said) with 7,000 or
*more horse, wold have taken the citie, and by canon forcing open a
gate entered, and some fewe before him, but the streetes were strowed
with harrowes, covered with strawe, also with frames of tables, buffet
stooles, &c.; and the houses on both sides flanked with muskatiers, the*

**Contradicted.** *women being readie prepared with great stones, brick-battes, on the top of
the houses, to kill or make disturbance; but the King crying " On, on "
for hast, because of the country and the Lord Brookes army, the horsemen fell among the harrowes, ij. pieces were discharged upon them, the
flankers and women played theire partes, so that the company fled, and
the King followed, some of his guard slaine just by him, and of others
Colonell Lunsford and two or three hundred, Captain Leg taken
prisoner, &c. (sic dicitur).*

The truth is (if bookes be true, and if Coventry men at Sturbridge
fayer-time say true) that the King was not there.  But his army was,
and did not enter the towne, but shot into it, yet kild only one man
that vaulted himself on the wall.  The towne issued out, and slue
diverse, chasing the rest, who went to a more four miles of, at which
place the Lord Brooke's company came up to them, and there was a
slaughter of diverse (about forty or sixty), and the rest fledde.  One

---

[a] Gifford-hall, Stoke by Neyland, co. Suffolk.

only slaine, on the Lord Brooke's side, that began the slaughter, (*sic dicitur*) all done with canon.

Monday, August the 22, the King's standerd set up at Notingham. Standard set up at Nottingham.
On Friday the 2. of September, the earle of Essex went out of Earle of Essex London with his companies.

September 21, at Bury, the booke of Portsmouth rendered by Portsmouth. colonel Goring to the Parliament, upon composition.[a]  A booke of a fight at Sherborne castle.[b]  A booke of two letters, one from the Vice-chancellor of Oxford, &c., to theire chancellor the noble lord Oxford Erle. of Pembroke, imploring defense against the injuries of the common soldiers feared, &c.; the other his answer,—That this wold have beene done before they had opposed the Parliament; but nowe, putting themselves in the posture of schollers againe, he wold be a frend as he cold.[c]

I sawe there diverse horsemen to goe into Lincolnshire, who accompanied sir Christopher Wrey [d] from the White Heart out of towne, a litle way towards London, by Hargate house, &c.  The Parliament colors at Bury. Lieftenant's colors were an armed arme holding up a sword, and this word about it, *The warre is just that is necessary.*

This day I heard of a late insurrection in Kent, (such perhaps as Sir Edward Deering's house was about a month since at Long Melford,[e] where the lady Savage her house was defaced, &c. and pillaged,) wherein sir Edward Deering's house was pulled downe, &c.

I cold relate diverse things that make me aston'de, partly delivered by his Majestie's partie, partly occasionally drawne from the Parliament in answer to that party, when I observe the unexpected working. (Those I saw this day at Bury:)  1. His Majestie (as we are told in print,) demandeth a pardon for the Malignant party.  Thus it

---

[a] " An exact relation of the passages which happened at Portsmouth at the late siege." 4to. London, 1642.

[b] " Exceeding true News from Boston, Sherbourne castle, &c." 4to. London, 1642.

[c] Both printed in Rushworth, pt. iii. vol. ii. pp. 11-13.

[d] Of Ashley, co. Lincoln.        [e] See p. 121.

worketh.    I hope the King will not desire it, or the Parliament grant it; for who then shall pay all the vast charges that the land hath been put to? (which must be paid).    2. It is complained of, that the Parliament hath used all indefatigable care and forcast in this busines.    Doth not the multitude say, O noble Parliament?    3. The Parliament saith that the King, by proclaming the earl of Essex and his adherent traytors, hath put the whole body of the land out of his protection.    Judge what it worketh in the people.

About October 10, my brother sawe a booke that shewed the grounds of suspition that the old marquesse Hamilton and king James were both poysoned by the duke and his mother, &c.    A large and well pend discourse.[a]

[ACCOMMODATION.]

The Parliament cries " Armie;" the King sayes " No!"
The newe Lieftenants crie, " Marche on, let us goe."
The Citizens and Roundheades crie, " So, so."
The People, all amazed, crie, " Where is the foe ? "
The Scottes that stand behind the dore crie " Boh !"
Here stay a while, and you shall know.
The King stands still, faster then they can goe ;
For if, by force of armes, the King prevailes,
He is invited to a tyrannie ;
But if, by strength of Parliament, he failes,
We heape continuall warres upon posteritie.
Then he that is not for accommodation
Loves neither God, nor Church, nor King, nor Nation.

These verses, I believe, were made before that the Earle of Essex went forth, and may be conceived to be a secret taxing of the Parliament, for arming of men against the King, when he protested not to intende warre against the Parliament.    Indeed if the Parliament

---

[a] By George Eglisham, or Eglisemmius, a Scotchman ; it was originally written in Latin, and published in 1626, but translated and entitled " The Forerunner of Revenge ; being two Petitions, one to the King and the other to the Parliament; wherein is expressed divers actions of the late earl (*sic*) of Buckingham, especially concerning the death of king James and the marquess of Hamilton, supposed by poyson." 4to. London, 1642.    It is reprinted both in the Harleian Miscellany, vol. ii. and in the Somers Tracts, vol. v.

had not sufficient groundes of a contrary practise, by the Malignant side with the King appeering at Hull and elsewhere, they had deserved to be taxed; yet it was litle witte in the composer to taxe that high court, and further what knavery was in it I leave to be judged by others.   I conceive (as the Parliament) that his Majestie is abused, and I conceive of the Malignant party (some at the least) as of cheators, that desire to be believed, till they have fully gulled the foole they have in handling.   Legge of Brandon said, " Believe it."

Thus I have written in leaning to others, who perhaps may have hit the veine of him that wrote the verses.   But yet I, in another charitable way, (because the author is unknowne,) can construe thus, " Then he," &c. *vers. ultimo*, viz. That desires not a peaceable accommodation, Loves not God, Church, King, nor Nation.   Who loves not the Parliament, loves not the Nation.   Who loves not the King and Parliament, *in the way on foote from the Parliament*, loves none of all.   The Parliament that be for the King, prince, &c. with the safety of the nation, have given theire word and promise (which is the word of the kingdome, not easily violated or to be abused,) for His Majestie's safetie and honour.   Some yet call the Parliament side Roundheads, who be themselves, in requitall, called Malignants.   (They wold not have the title of the father of all malignants, I dare say;) but what title they deserve, let themselves judge who hate reformation, and wold bring in tyrannie.   I followe the author of the former verses.

About October 22, there was a Declaration from both houses,[a] setting forth His Majestie's late dealing in Ireland, to the encouragement of rebels, his sending for foraine aid to Hamburgh, Denmarke, and neerer neighbors: his commissions to diverse named papists, to gather up men in England against the Parliament, &c.

October 23, was the bataile neere Kinton in Warwickshire, The battail neer Kinton.

[a] Rushworth, pt. iii. vol. ii. p. 26.

towards Banbury in Oxfordshire.  About this battaile, the lord Wharton's, Mr. Stroud's, the earl of Pembroke's, the lord Saye's, and th earl of Holland's speeches at the Guildhall, London, be extant.[a]  Th lord Wharton and Mr. Stroud were of the Parliament army, in thi fight, who related to the lord mayor to this effect.  The fight wa in the place recited, about a place called Edge-hill, October 23 The King's forces came in the morning; the battaile began (in heate about three or four in the afternoon.  The erle of Essex' cannon began first on the assailants.  The King's forces had the advantage of number much, and of wind and hill.  At the first onset, the lord Wharton's regiment of horse, and three others of the left wing fled prince Rupert's company pursued them, slaying many and plunder ing the wagons of the erle, and diverse captaines.  The erle's company fought stoutly, and with the losse of about 300 men, slewe 3,000, tooke the King's standerd, sir Henry [Edmund] Verney being slaine.  They tooke the erle of Linsey, the generall (who is since dead of his hurt); also the lord Willoughby, his sonne.  They tooke colonell Vavasor and Lunsford (who they say is dead), whose brother was slaine.  The erle stood upon the field that night, Moonday and part of Tuisday.  The King's company shewed themselves, Moonday morning, on an hill, but approched not.  The erle tooke four pieces of ordnance, and many colours.  *In the same booke is inserted,* among the speeches, a Speech of His Majestie to his soldiers, ex- pressing what he had done and protested for the Parliament, and the protestant religion, inciting to fight couragiously, *saying that battailes successe shold manifest his innocency.*  The lord Sayes close was to excite the Londoners to be readie and forward, in pursuing the victory; (wherof one said, he never saw more done by God, and lesse by man,) using this persuasion, " Men in a common fire run and helpe to quench, never asking who shall pay for theire worke."

15,000 to
8,000 or 9.

See one accident
about this fight
175.[b]

---

[a] " Eight Speeches, spoken in Guildhall, October 27, 1642, by the lord Wharton," &c 4to. London, 1642.

[b] See p. 129 *infra.*

It is since reported that many of the King's part are fled, *and* Many loades
*many wounded* are dead at Oxford; and that the King's part suffered were carried away.
more losse then before. *Too much.*[a] Upon the 21 of November, it
remained as a doubt whether prince Rupert were not slaine (who
returned from plundering to the fight): of whom some say he was cut
of by the middle, others he was beate of his horse; others that his
plume and helmet were taken up out of the bloud; others generally
that a George was found among the slaine, supposed to be his, for he
was lately advanced extraordinary to be knight of the Garter. They
suppose this is concealed in policy, and that still a prince Rupert is
feined in the campe.

November 2, came forth another (the last) Parliament Remonstrance, in answer to his Majestie's answer about Hull busines. It is
full, and was kept till now by reason of weighte affayres on foote.
(Dr. Archbishop of Yorke penned the King's answer.) In the
remonstrance, I observed a record of the manner of coronation. The
oath being given on a scaffold, by Canterbury, the said archbishop
turneth to the people on ech side of the scaffold, saying " The oath
is taken; will you gladly accept this King to reigne over you ?"
Theire consent endes the busines.

November 21, I saw at Mr. Prattes at Hockwold,[b] " Speciall Another fight.
Passages," from November 8 to 15, where it is said Sir Eveling [c]
spake to the lower house, that he was sory that he was set as a marke
by the King, &c., to stay the accommodation; (we had heard that
six were appointed for delivery of a Parliament message, and one
was proclaimed Traytor (for an hindrance) by a newe wet proclamation, for his hindering the commiss. of array, &c). The Parliament commons consulted, and sent the other five, leaving him to goe
or not, *pro libitu.*[d] Wednesday (I suppose) they went with a

---

[a] Added afterwards.　　　　　　　　[b] Grimshoe hundred, co. Norfolk.

[c] Sir John Evelyn.

[d] Evelyn had been excepted by name, in the King's proclamation for pardon to the
county of Wiltshire, and therefore the King refused to receive him.

Petition to consider of prevention of bloudshed, to desire establish-
ment of religion, lawes, liberties of subjects, priviledges of parliament.[a]
The King accepts it, delayes answer for a while as needing no hast.
On Friday or Thursday, his Majestie makes answer with deepe protestations about religion, lawes, &c., *pro more solito.*[b]  On Saturday it
is said, (notwithstanding the same protestations,) he and his army
came in a misty morning betimes, from Colnebrooke to Brainford,
six miles from London, where sir Denzill Hollis' Regiment of
Butchers, that had fought stoutly in the former battail, were billeted;
and there began an hote fight from ten to three *pomer.* diverse
being slaine; and that the King's side plundered the towne, and
tooke linnen, brasse, victuals, &c., and left the towne naked.    That
the King's armie went to Kingston-upon-Thames; and there through
fayre wordes was entertained, yet might have been kept out from
coming over the bridge.    That a pinnace on the Thames, comming
up with amunition, was shot at and defended stoutly by the mariners,
till at length they were forced to flie by the boate, yet left a traine;
and in the escape fired her there, lest the King's side shold enjoy her
carriage, &c. I there also sawe the letter of sir Corn. V.,[d] who agrees
to the battaile, and the King's comming in person on Saturday,
affirming that there was a sore fight, and that two small Parliamentary supplies came, ere the skirmish ended; that 100 or 200
were slaine,—that the Parliament army was here on Sunday morne,
—that the King's army, (by some suspected fault,) was not set upon,
but suffered to depart, and goe over the Thames to Kingston in
Surrey; that the Parliament army is 25,000, the King's but 9,000;
that the Cavaliers killed one woman's child of three days ould before
her face, and then killed her; that a gentleman, a German of his
acquaintance, rode from London to Brainford to see the towne; and

---

[a] Printed in Clarendon's History of the Rebellion, vol. ii. p. 103.
[b] A mistake.   It was returned in a few hours. Ibid. p. 104.
[c] Brentford.
[d] Probably Sir Cornelius Vermuyden.

returning, told him that of all the plundered townes he had seen in Germany, he had seen not one so ruinde and defaced as Brainford. That all the townes between Oxford and Brainford are also plundered: that the Parliament resolves an irrevocable pursuite of the spoylers, &c.; that 4,000 newe horse were readie for that service.

In the Passages, I remember it was said that, whereas it was desired that some saylors might goe with the erle of Warwicke, the maister of the Trinity House at Detford gave contrary charge, who is therefore a delinquent, and his office taken from him, &c.   I was told of some older newes, viz: a daughter of Mr. Asty once of Feltw. Nich.[a] in the house now the lord Bankes' (who married Mr. Cradock, minister, and her brother is parson of Wrentham,[b] by Henham), wrote to her father that, lately in these times, her husband, mr. Cradocke, had intelligence in the night, that certaine Cavaliers that night wold kill him; he fled out of bed, went not in the high way, but over hedges, by-pathes, &c., appointing his man to meet him with an horse.   The Cavaliers came, raged that they cold not find him; the wife gave good wordes; they threatned to kill her; she entreated, and avowed that he was fled, she knew not whether; they plundered, tooke a chest of linnen, and sought for more; but some from the parliamentary quarters came to rescue, and beate a drum; so the Cavaliers fled, yet tooke all the horses of Mr. Cradocke, and that linnen.   Mr. Cradocke and his company be gotten to Coventry, and dare not use theire parsonage.

Mr. Cradocke, Warwickshire.

Mr. Snelling senior told me at Brandon, November 11, that he had a kinsman married, who, with fifteen more yonkers (some of the innes of court), went on pleasure from London to see the Campe, and were there October 22: so then they stood as spectators, October 23,

---

[a] Feltwell, consisting of the parishes of St. Mary and St. Nicholas consolidated, hundred of Grimshoe, co. Norfolk.

[b] The baptisms of three children of "Robert Asty, preacher of God's word," in 1639-1642, are given from the registers of Wrentham, in Davy's Suffolk Collections, Addit. MS. 19,083, f. 219.

CAMD. SOC.                    s

till the King's side went downe, and then they gave aid to it, and were cut of, thirteen of them.  His kinsman escaping, wrote this to his wife, then at Thetford with Mr. Snelling.

Another thing was told by mr. Chaplen, at Downham, November 30, that one of the King's side, a Yorkeshire man, was in the fight, and heard many cursing and blaspheming, with imprecations against the Roundheads, whom he sawe perish in the middest of theire oathes, &c.  He observed three things that went neere him.  The King's side wanted powder, and going to one wagon for powder that was blowen up, and so a second, with the losse of many men; and one piece of ordnance, a greate one, a murderer, &c., at the first shoote, burst in many pieces, and hurt many of theire owne, &c.  These made him resolve a departure from that side, which he made by helpe of a frend, who bought the Parliament colours, by which he returned home safe.  The same told us that the good lord Willoughby of Parham was strangely delivered; he tooke physicke that day at Kinton, not thinking of a fight.  The captaine that brought up his company brought them close up, and then fled to the other side, shot of his pistoll, and cried "for the King."  The men not brought of perished.  This had light on the lord, if he had beene there.  He being warned, fled on horse backe, with his physicke in his body, to a farmer's house three or four miles of, and in a barne retired himselfe and escaped.  Quere.

A ship taken between Boston and Hull with 1,500 armes, 160 barrelles of gunpowder.  Boston men ride out and fetch in such as speake against the Parliament, causing some to be sent to the Parliament, some to be bailed for appeerance, &c., as theire fault deserves—some imprisonment.

<table>
<tr><td>Cheapside Crosse.<br>Another called England's petitioner.</td><td>In the beginning of May 1643, Cheapside crosse was taken downe.  A booke intituled " Questions resolved and Propositions tending to Accommodation and Agreement between the King, &c."</td></tr>
</table>

First question.

1. Whether a King be ordeined of God for the welfare of the

people, or the people appointed subjects to the King, for the honour
and pleasure of a King.

2. Whether a King maketh or imposeth lawes upon a people, or
the lawes and antient native and ancient customes of the land doe
erect and establish the throne and crowne of a King.

3. What power or prerogative the King hath, *supra*, *præter*, or
*contra legem terræ.*

Nolumus pre-<br>rogativam regis<br>disputari.

4. What power or priviledge the high court of Parliament hath,
assembled as the representative body of the kingdome.

Barones nolu-<br>mus leges<br>Angliæ immu-<br>tari.

ᵃ Discovering six sorts of Malignants.

1. All Papists, &c.

ᵃ So in MS.

# INDEX.

ABBOT, George, archbishop of Canterbury, 75
Adams, Mr. 83
Admiral, lord, *vide* Buckingham, duke of
Aldermanbury, 80
Alexander, William, 56
Almanacs, prophetic, 102
Alps, 87
America, 32
Amsterdam, 34, 42, 96, 117
Anglesey, Charles Villiers, earl of, 51
Antwerp, 96
Aragon, 121
Archduchess, *vide* Isabella Clara Eugenia
Argyle, Archibald Campbell, earl of, 3
Arinarguers, 36
Aristotle, 115
Arminian, 35, 42
Arminianism, 35, 40
Arundel, Thomas Howard, earl of, lord chief justice in Eyre, 23, 92
Arundel, Henry Frederick, earl of, lord Maltravers, 3, 88
Arundel, Elizabeth countess of, 3
Ashton, captain, 42
Astley, sir Jacob, 7, 86
Asty, Mr. 129
Asty, Mr. daughter of, 129
Audley, lord, *vide* Castlehaven, earl of
Austria, 74

Austria, house of, 59
Ayers, Thomas, 64

Babel, 102
Babylon, 111
Ball, Dr. Richard, 84
Baltic sea, 67
Banbury, 126
Banks, sir J. attorney-general and lord chief justice, 77, 129
Baracke, brother (Barclay ?) 42
Barret, Mr. 35, 38, 44
Barton mills, 48, 67
Bastwick, Dr. John, 82, 99
Bavaria, Maximilian duke of, 59
Bayly (Lewis ?), bishop (of Bangor ?) 76
Bealings, sir Henry, 76
Beauchamp's court, 30
Beckham, 69
Bedford, 83
Bedford, Francis Russell, earl of, 94
Bedingfield, 24
Beecher, sir Thomas, 98
Beecher, sir William, 101
Beke, Henry, 64
Bell Sound, 64
Bennet college, 70
Bergen-op-Zoom, 62
Berkeley, sir Robert, judge, 85, 113

Berkshire, 1, 90, 91
Berwick, 88
Binion, Mr. 121
Bohemia, 38, 67
Bolingbroke, Oliver St. John, earl of, 94
Booker's prophetic almanac, 102
Boston, 53, 86, 130
Bramston, sir Jo. 85
Brandon, 11, 49, 60, 125, 129
Breda, 82
Brentford, 128, 129
Brett, sir Alexander, 21
Britain, 29, 38, 88
Bristol, 17
Bristol, John Digby, earl of, 100
British heretics, 38
Brooke, Fulk Greville, lord, 30
Brooke, Robert Greville, lord, 94, 98, 101, 122, 123
Brooke, lady, 101
Browning, Nathan, 61, 68
Buchanan (Beucanian), John, 42
Bucke, rev. James, 83, 84
Bucke, rev. ——, 66
Buckingham, George Villiers, duke of, 1, 3, 7—12, 14—20, 25—34, 42, 124
Buckingham, Katherine duchess of, 27, 28, 32
Buckingham, Mary Villiers, countess of, 124
Buckinghamshire, 83, 112
Burgundians, 81
Burton, Henry, 5, 37, 82, 99
Bury St. Edmund's, 6, 8, 41, 48, 53, 54, 60, 61, 62, 68, 81, 83, 121, 123
Bushell, Philip, 76
Butts, Dr. 70
Cadiz, 1, 22

Cales, vide Cadiz
Calvin, John, reformer, 62
Calvinists, 67
Cambridge, 3, 6, 10, 34, 51, 52, 55, 56, 63, 70, 79, 99, 115
Cambridge, earl of, vide Hamilton, marquis
Cambridgeshire, 83
Canada, 37
Canterbury Bell, the, 117
Canterbury, archbp. vide Abbot and Laud
Canwick (or Stanwick,) rev. Mr. 103.
Carleton, George, bishop of Chichester, 5, 6
Carlos, Don, vide Colonna
Cassal, 87
Castlehaven, earl of, Mervin Touchet, lord Audley, 60
Castleton, sir William, 121
Catlin, Mr. 69
Chaderton, Dr. 99
Chalcedon, bishop of, vide Smith, Richard
Chamberlain, lord, vide Lindsey, earl of
Chaplen, Mr. 130
Charles I. 1—4, 7, 9—12, 14—19, 25, 26, 28, 29, 32—39, 42, 44, 46, 47, 49, 51—54, 56, 70, 75, 76, 80, 82, 85, 87—101, 104, 106—108, 113, 114, 118, 120—131
Charles II., prince, 52—55, 114, 125
Cheapside Cross, 130
Cheshire, 8
Chichester, bishop of, vide Carleton
Christian IV., king of Denmark, 7, 10, 12, 17, 38, 43
Churchwardens, 51, 52
Cleaver, William, 117
Clement VIII., pope, 87
Clerke, ——, 15
Clerkenwell, 14

Cleveland, 59

Cleye, 23

Coke, sir Edward, lord chief justice of the king's bench, 2, 3, 8

Colchester, 121

Colnbrook, 128

Colonna, Don Carlos de, Spanish Ambassador, 56, 59, 83

Commons, House of, 4, 16, 40, 50, 98, 100, 104, 105, 111, 112, 119, 120, 127, 128

Condé, Henry de Bourbon, prince of, 113

Constance, queen of Poland, 61

Conway, Edward, lord secretary of state, 21

Corbet, Richard, bishop of Oxford, 43, 55, 70, 71

Coriton, Mr. 40

Cosin, Dr. John, bishop of Durham, 35

Cotton, Mr. 53

Coventry, 122, 129

Coventry, sir Thomas, lord keeper, 3

Couper, Mr. 58

Cradock, Mr. 129

Cradock, Mrs. 129

Craven, William lord, 86

Crewe, sir Randolph, chief justice of the king's bench, 7, 8

Crofts, Francis, 67

Croke, sir George, justice of the king's bench, 85, 90

Crosby, master, 73

Crow, sir Sackville, 34

Cudworth, widow, 80

Dalham, 61, 110

Dancer, at Lynn, verses on, 73

Danes, 38, 104

Dawes, John, 64

Denbigh, William Fielding, earl of, 15, 17

Denmark, 82, 125

Denmark, king of, *vide* Christian IV.

Dennington, 45, 61

Deptford, 129

Derbyshire, 8, 9

Dering, sir Edward, 123

Diglets, Mr. 24

Dod, John, 117

Dorset, Edward Sackville, earl of, 17, 31

Downham, 121, 130 ; ministers' house at, ix.

Drapier, 39

Drury, sir Drew, 32

Ducke, Dr. 99

Dudley, sir Edmund, 109

Dunkirk, 2

Dunkirk ship, 55

Dunkirkers, 2, 9, 18, 43

Dutch, *vide* Hollanders

East Dereham, 49

Edgehill, 126

Edgar, launched, 83

Edward I., 97

Egelfred, Ethelred, king, 104

Elden, 67

Elizabeth, queen, 30, 39, 98

Elizabeth, queen of Bohemia, 17, 19

Ellingham, 48, 49

Elliot, sir John, 40

Elmswell, 60

Ely, bishop of, *vide* Wren, Matthew

Emmanuel college, 80, 99

Empson (Simpson), sir Richard, 109

England, 1, 6, 8, 13, 18, 25, 39, 40, 53, 56, 59, 63, 66, 76, 80, 82, 90, 93, 95, 97, 114, 125

English, 13, 14, 21, 25, 27, 29, 30, 32, 46, 49, 63, 66, 75, 87, 90, 103, 104

Epirus, 74

Eriswell, 31

Essex, 2, 5, 7, 14, 83

Essex, Robert Devereux, earl of, 9, 94, 123, 124, 126

Europe, 86, 87

Evelyn, sir John, 127

Exchange, Royal, 33

Exchequer, 51, 90, 104

Exeter, William Cecill, earl of, 94

Fakeley, William, 64

Falkland, Henry Cary, viscount, 47, 75, 104

Faringdon, 90

Felton, John, 25, 26, 27, 28, 29, 30, 33, 34

Feltwell, 123

Ferdinand II. emperor of Germany, 36, 40, 59, 63, 65, 67, 81, 82

Ferdinand III. emperor, 59, 67, 82, 113

Fielding, viscount, *vide* Denbigh, earl, 15, 33

Finborough, 60

Finch, sir John, lord chief justice of common pleas and lord keeper, 34, 77, 99, 107, 108, 117

Flanders, 83

Fleet prison, 47, 121

Flegg, 56

Flemish, 38

Flinde, William, 116

Fountain, Mr. 39

Fortune, 58

France, 1, 9, 10, 11, 12, 13, 22, 32, 39, 41, 44, 46, 47, 50, 59, 73, 75, 81, 82, 113, 121

France, king of, *vide* Louis XIII.

Frederic V. king of Bohemia, 34, 38, 54, 65, 68, 69, 70

French, 7, 8—13, 15, 20, 21, 32, 33, 37, 39, 44, 46, 98, 121

Friedland, Albertus Wenceslaus Wallenstein, duke of, 7

Fryer, colonel, 28

Gabor, Bethlehem, 44

Games, Mr. 45

Garie, Mr. 69

Garnet, father, 102

Geneva, 73, 117

Germany, 13, 59, 73, 75, 77, 86, 98, 113, 129

Germany, emperor, of *vide* Ferdinand

Germany, states of, 59

Gilly, Mr. daughter of, 60

Gohogan, Arthur, 75

Goliah, 102

Goodfellow, Robert, 64

Goodler, captain William, 64

Goring, colonel, 32, 123

Goths, 74

Grantham, vicar of, 80

Gravesend, 53

Grebner, Paul, 65, 68

Greece, 74

Greene, Mr. 62

Greenland, Mr. 63, 64

Greenwich, 75

Gregory XV. 109

Grimes Hall, 11

Groll, 10

Guelderland, 10

Guildhall, 126

Gustavus Adolphus, king of Sweden, 38, 43, 56, 59, 61, 63, 65—70, 73—75

Hadleigh, 81

Hales, 24, 55, 56

Halesworth, 58, 66

Hamburgh, 96, 123
Hamilton, James Douglas, 2nd marquis of, 124
Hamilton, James Douglas, 3rd marquis of, 54, 61, 65
Hanse towns, 67
Hargate, 121, 123
Harleston, 66
Harrison, Mr. 86
Harvey, Francis, judge, 24, 62
Harwich, 2
Hayman, sir Peter, 40
Heape, Jo. 29
Heath, sir Robert, lord chief justice of the common pleas, 63, 68, 77
Henham, 7, 66, 129
Henrietta Maria, queen, 1, 11, 12, 32, 39, 49, 54, 56, 70, 88
Henry IV. king of France, 12
Henry, prince of Bohemia, 34, 35
Henry V. 38
Henry of Huntingdon, 104
Herbert, sir Edward, attorney-general, 121
Hereford, 75
Hertford, William Seymour, earl of, 94
Hertfordshire, 83
Hertogensbusche, 41, 43
Heveningham, sir John, 8, 14
Heylin, Dr. 80, 107
Higham, Mr. 27
Hobart, sir Miles, 40; *vide* Hubberd
Hockwold, 125
Holborn, London, 84
Holborn, Mr. 85
Holland, 30, 32, 33, 66, 82
Holland, Henry Rich, earl of, 12, 25, 46, 75, 80, 126
Hollanders, 9, 11, 14, 27, 33, 35, 38, 41, 43, 45, 46, 59, 60, 62, 64, 82, 83, 113

Hollis, sir Denzill, 40, 128
Holton, 58
Honington, 82
Howard, lord, 94
Howlet, Mr. 11
Hubberd, Mr. 48
Hubberd, sir John, 48
Hughenden, 112
Hull, 65, 125, 127, 130
le Hunt, sir George, 61
Hutchinson, sir Thomas, 111
Hutton, sir Richard, justice of common pleas, 86
Hyde, sir Nicholas, lord chief justice of the king's bench, 8, 48, 49, 62, 63

Imperialists, 81
Indies, 50
Indies, East, 14, 33
Indies, West, 33, 43, 45
Ipswich, 2, 23, 45, 62, 82, 99
Ireland, 46, 60, 62, 75, 76, 98, 120, 121, 125
Irishmen, 14, 38, 70, 75, 94
Isabella Clara Eugenia, archduchess and governess of the Spanish Netherlands, 39
Italian, 84
Italy, 46, 87
Ixworth, 49, 82

James I. 3, 4, 11, 26, 30, 34, 50, 71, 125
James, duke of York, 75
James, Mr. 48
Jenkinson, Mr. 62
Jen[ner], T. 29
Jermy, 83, 84
Jermyn, sir Thomas, 61
Jerusalem, 103

Jesuits, 13, 14, 33, 39, 46, 61, 62, 66, 75, 98, 119
Jones, judge, 85
Jordan, 42
Judges, 50, 62, 85, 90, 104, 105, 107
Juxon, Dr. William, bishop of London, 75, 80

Keene, Mr. 49
Keeper, lord, *vide* Coventry and Finch
Keinton, 125, 130
Kellett, Richard, 64
Kent, 33, 70, 117, 123
Kesgrave, 45
Kilmallock, Dominic Sarsfield, viscount, 76
Kingston-upon-Thames, 128
Kirke, captain, 32, 37
Kn. John, 72

Lackford, 66, 67
Lambe, Dr. 17, 20, 26, 31
Lambeth, 35, 37, 81, 90, 101
Lancashire, 8, 9
Landguard fort, 2, 7, 62
Langer fort, *vide* Landguard fort
Lapland, 66
Laud, William, bishop of London, archbishop of Canterbury, 35, 36, 56, 75, 82, 109, 115, 118, 119; verses on, 109, 117
Laud, Mr. 58
Laxfield, 45
Leader, William, 37
Lees, co. Essex, 45
Legge, Mr. 125
Legge, captain, 122
Leicestershire, 9
Leighton, Dr. Alexander, 53, 54, 55, 99
Leipsic, 67, 70
Lennox, Esme Stuart, duke of, 3, 54

Ley, sir James, lord chief justice of the king's bench, earl of Marlborough, 8
Lilly, William, 117
Lincoln, Tom of, 117
Lincoln, Theophilus Clinton, earl of, 9, 94
Lincolnshire, 9, 10, 48, 60, 83, 123
Lincoln's inn, 46, 70
Lindsey, Robert Bertie, lord Willoughby, earl of, lord chamberlain, 30, 126
Lisbon, 75
Litcham, 81
Lithgo, 73
Littleport, 63
Littleton, Edward, recorder, king's solicitor, afterwards lord Lyttleton, 77
Loddon, 56, 57
Lombard street, 111
London, 1, 5, 11, 13, 14, 16, 17, 23, 27, 31, 32, 35, 36, 39, 41, 45—47, 49, 50, 52, 53, 55, 56, 58, 62, 65, 70, 75, 76, 80—82, 88, 93, 98, 100, 103, 121, 123, 128, 129
London, bishop of, *vide* Laud
London bridge, 70
London, lords mayor of,
    sir James Campbell, 42
    sir Hugh Hammersley, 18
    sir Richard Deane, 18
    sir Robert Ducie, 54
    sir Richard Gurney, 126
Londoners, 18, 53, 126
London, Tower of, 2, 8, 9, 14, 18, 60, 70, 81
Long Melford, 121, 123
Lords, house of, 98, 113, 119
Lorraine, Charles duke of, 65, 77, 78
Lorraine, house of, 77, 78, 81
Lorraine, Nicholas Francis, duke of, 77, 78
Lorrainers, 81

Loudon, John Campbell, earl of, chancellor of Scotland, 88
Louis XIII. king of France, 1, 8, 9, 15, 54, 59, 77, 78, 81, 86, 87
Lovelace, John lord, 94
Lowestoft, 55
Lucifer, 38
Lunsford, colonel, 123, 126
Lushington, Dr. 44, 77
Luther, 62
Lynn, 55, 60, 73, 81
Lyttleton, *see* Littleton.

Machiavelli, 109
Maddeson, Mr. 22, 23, 24
Magdeburg, 61, 62, 63
Mainwaring, Dr. Roger, bishop of St. David's, 17, 37
Maltravers, lord, 2 ; *vide* Arundel
Manchester, Henry Montagu, earl of, 8
Mandeville, viscount, 94
Mannock, sir Francis, 122
Mansfeldt, Ernest count of, 7
Marie de Medicis, 12, 39, 54, 59, 98
Marlborough, James Ley, earl of, 8
Marlow, 99
Marshalsea prison, 8, 14
Martin, Mr. 46, 122
Martlesham, 23
Mary, princess of Orange, 63, 113
Mass, verses on the, 118
Maud, Mr. 41
Melford, 121
Mentz, 68
Methwold, 69
Mexico, 47
Ministers, 51, 52, 69, 80, 111, 112, 113, 120, 122

Mohun, captain, 90
Mondeford, 44
Montague, Richard, bishop of Chichester and Norwich, 5, 6, 37
Montagu, Walter, 25
Montpesson, sir Giles, 110
Morocco and Fez, king of, *vide* Muley Scheck
Moscow, 68
Muley Scheck, emperor of Morocco, 83
Mulgrave, Edmund Sheffield, earl of, 94
Musgrave, Mr. 48, 49

Nantes, 86
Naples, 113
Nassau Liegen, John count of, 69
Navarre, 81
Nehemiah, 103
Netherlands, 7, 56, 75
Newcastle-upon-Tyne, 81, 92, 93, 98
New Churchman, The (verses), 78
New England, 53, 54, 80
Newgate, 76
Newmarket, 56
Nivella, Jean de, 73
Norfolk, 1, 2, 6, 8, 10, 12, 13, 14, 16, 51, 56, 67, 68
Normans, 104
Normansell, 31
North, Dudley lord, 94
North, Mr. 121
Northampton, 86
Northamptonshire, 9, 83
Norton, Mr. 58
Norwich, 5, 6, 31, 37, 52, 56, 57, 62, 63, 67, 77, 80, 82, 83
Nottingham, 123
Nova Francia, 32
Noye, sir William, attorney-general, 76

Orange, Frederick Henry prince of, 10, 43, 44, 62, 113

Orange, William prince of, 113

Orleans, 81

Orleans, Gaston duke of, 63, 77

Overbury, sir Thomas, 72

Overton, Henry, 112

Oxborough, 23, 24

Oxford, 1, 2, 6, 44, 71, 127

Oxford, vice-chancellor of, 123

Oxfordshire, 90, 125

Paine, Mr. 11, 45

Palatinate, 12, 56, 59, 65, 67, 69

Palatine, elector, Charles Louis, 81, 82, 86, 88

Palatine, prince, vide Frederick V.

Palsgrave, vide Frederick V.

Papists, 1, 2, 3, 22, 43, 60, 61, 93, 98, 117 —119, 121, 125, 131

Paris, 81

Parliament, 1, 2, 3, 6, 7, 12, 14—18, 23, 30, 35, 36, 39, 40, 47, 55, 88, 90, 91, 94, 95, 98, 99, 101, 103, 104, 106, 108, 110—114, 119—121, 123—131

Parliament, verses on the dissolution 1640, 88

Partridge, Jo. 63

Peck, Mr. 69

Pelham, Edward, 64

Pembroke Hall, 84

Pembroke, Mary countess of, 54

Pembroke, Philip Herbert, earl of, 36, 123, 101, 126

Pembroke, William Herbert, earl of, [read " as, Pembroke,"] 51

Pennington, alderman, 111

Pennington, captain, 10

Perkins, Mr. 54

Philip II. of Spain, 66

Philip IV. king of Spain, 59, 97

Philips, sir Robert, 2

Phœbus, 43

Pilsworth, 76

Plague, the, 50, 51, 52, 55, 56, 60, 62

Playfair, Mr. 58

Plymouth, 1, 31

Poland, 43, 58, 61

Poland, queen of, vide Constance

Polychronicon, 103

Pomerania, Bugislaus duke of, 59

Pope's head alley, 111

Popes, vide Gregory XV., Urban VIII.

Portsmouth, 10, 14, 25, 31, 32, 123

Portugal, 113, 121

Prague, 65, 67

Pratt, a murderer, 70

Pratt, Mr. Osbert, 16, 37, 49, 127

Prince, heathen, 47

Privy councillors, 28, 30, 47, 50, 76, 92, 94

Prophecies, 36, 103 ; of Grebner, 65, 68

Prophetic almanac, 102

Protestants, 9, 13, 46, 60, 67, 77, 79, 119, 126

Prynne, William, 38, 42, 70, 82, 90, 99

Puritans, 45, 55, 118

Pye, sir ——, 62

Pym, Mr. 42

Queen regent, vide Marie de Medicis

R. sir W. 72

Ramsey, Mr. 50

Ravens, Dr. 34

Reade, Mr. 104

Reading, 1

Rednall, 66

Reedham ferry, 57

Reeve, sir Edward, judge, 101

Reimingham, 56

Rhé, island of, 10, 11, 13, 14, 20, 21, 22, 31, 42

Rhætia, 87

Rich, sir Charles, 21

Richardson, sir Thomas, lord chief justice of the king's bench, 62, 63, 68

Richelieu, Armand John du Plessis, cardinal and duke of, 73, 86, 87

Riddlesworth, 11

Ripon, 100

Rochelle, 9, 10, 11, 13, 15, 17, 18, 25, 28, 30—33, 87

Rochellers, 11, 31

Rockland, 48

Rodolph, II. emperor of Austria, 66

Roe, [Rolfe,] sir Thomas, 68

Rogers, Mr. 6

Romans, king of, *vide* Ferdinand III. emperor

Rome, 30, 38, 74, 80, 117—119

Rotterdam, 96

Rous, pedigree of, v

Rous, Anthony, junior, 45

Rous, Anthony, senior, vi, 61

Rous, Mr. Francis, of Essex, 5, 6

Rous, Mrs. 45

Rous, JOHN, biographical notices of, vii

Rous, sir John, of Henham, 7

Royston, 48, 87

Rupert, prince, 81, 86, 126, 127

Russia, 68

Rutland, George Manners, earl of, 94


St. Augustine, 116

St. Christopher's island, 14, 44, 46

St. Margaret's, Westminster, 98

St. Martin's, 10

St. Paul's church, 37, 53, 54, 70, 99, 101, 103

Salisbury, 70

Sallee, town of Barbary, 83

Savage, Elizabeth lady, 121, 122, 123

Saville, Thomas lord, 94

Savoy, 86

Savoyans, 81

Saxony, John George V. elector of, 36, 63, 65, 66, 67, 81

Say and Sele, William Fienes, viscount, 85, 94, 95, 98, 101, 126

Scholar's complaint, the, 115

Scotland, 56, 75, 86, 88, 95, 100, 114, 117

Scots, 12, 25, 59, 85, 86, 92, 93, 95, 97, 98, 99, 100, 102, 104, 110, 111, 113, 114, 124

Scott, 17, 20, 90, 109

Scott, Mr. 62

Scott, Thomas, 6

Scrope, Emmanuel lord, 51

Selden, 40

Shelford, Robert, 79

Sherborne castle, 123

Sherfield, Henry, 70

Shrewsbury, George Talbot, earl of, 8, 51

Silesia, 65

Skinner, Mr. 45

Smith, Richard, bishop of Chalcedon, 34, 39

Smithfield, 76

Snelling, Mr. senior, 49, 129, 130

Somersetshire, 90

Soubise, Alex. de Rohan, duke of, 11, 13

Southon, Martin, 46

Southwark, 90, 101

Spain, 1, 2, 9, 12, 22, 30, 32, 46, 47, 56, 59, 60, 66, 75, 98, 111, 113, 121

Spain, king of, *vide* Philip IV.

Spaniards, 5, 13, 29, 33, 35, 36, 43, 46, 50, 56, 81, 87
Speller, sir Henry, 98
Spinola, Ambrosius marquis, 2, 39
Spring, sir William, 49
Stamford, captain, 42
Stanley, Mr. 49
Stanwick, Mr. 103
Stockton, co. Norfolk, 58
Stokesby, 56, 57
Stoughton, Dr. 79
Strafford, Thomas Wentworth, earl of, 75, 104, 117
Strasburg, 66
Stroud, Mr. 40, 126
Sturbridge, 43, 55, 56, 65, 122
Stuteville, sir Martin, 61
Sudbury, 27, 99
Suffolk, 2, 7, 13, 14, 23, 27, 53, 61, 82, 83, 121
Suffolk, Theophilus Howard, earl of, 8
Suffolk, Thomas Howard, earl of, 3
Sunderland, Emmanuel Scrope, earl of, 10
Surrey, 129
Sutcliffe, Dr. Matthew, 5
Sutton, Mr. 31
Swaffham, 23, 51, 86
Sweden, 59, 82
Sweden, king of, *vide* Gustavus Adolphus
Swedes, 81, 110

Taylor, Mr. 44, 66
Temple, 41
Texel, 33
Thames, 9, 128
Theobalds, 75
Thetford, 6, 10, 11, 31, 34, 48, 49, 50, 67, 130
Thirston, 68

Tillot, widow, 60
Tilly, Johannes Tsercles, count of, 10, 61 62, 63, 67
Timperley, Mr. 22, 23
Townsend, sir Roger, 16, 48, 50
Trinity college, Cambridge, 68
Tubbing, Mr. 86
Turnbull, Mr. 84
Tyburn, 33, 76
Tynemouth, 98

Utting, William, 45
Urban VIII. 38, 47, 67, 77, 78, 115, 119

Valtoline, 32
Valentine, Mr. 40
Vandals, 74
Vavasour, colonel, 126
Venice, 32, 47
Verney, sir Henry, 126
Vermuyden, sir Cornelius, 128
Verses, 70-75, 77-80, 83, 84, 86-90, 101-3, 109-11, 115-119

Walderswick, 61
Wales, 9, 62
Waller, Mr. 113
Ward, Mr. 61
Ware, 70
Warner, 84
Warren, Mr. 66, 122
Warwick, Robert Rich, earl of, 7, 9, 14, 43, 44, 45, 94, 95, 98, 101, 129
Warwickshire, 125
Watton, 37
Weeting, 24, 45, 61 ; parsonage, ix
Wentworth, sir Thomas, *vide* Strafford, earl of

Wesel, 43
Westminster, 81, 86, 98
Westminster, dean of, 11, 31
Wharton, Philip lord, 94, 126
Whelp, burning of the ship, 55
White Lion prison, 90
White, Dr. Francis, bishop of Carlisle, Norwich, and Ely, almoner to Charles I. 37, 75
Whitehall, 15, 35, 44
Whitlow, Mr. 56, 57, 58
—— daughter of, 56, 57, 58
—— wife of, 57
Wickham Market, 45
Wilby, 84
Williams, Dr. John, bishop of Lincoln and archbishop of York, 80, 82, 98, 117, 127
Willoughby, Francis lord, 25, 30
Willoughby, lord, *vide* Lindsey, earl of
Willoughby of Parham, lord, 94, 126, 130
Wilton, 41
Wimbledon, Edward Cecill, viscount, 1
Windebank, sir Francis, secretary of state, 98, 104, 117, 197

Windsor, 92
Wingfield, sir Anthony, 32
Wintrop, Mr. 53
Wise, John, 64
Withipole, Mr. 23, 41
Withipole, sir William, 22, 23, 41
Woodbridge, 15, 22, 23, 45
Woodhouse, sir Thomas, 11
Woodstock, 71
Worlich, 58
Wotton, Thomas lord, 51
Wray, sir Christopher, 123
Wren, Matthew, bishop of Norwich and Ely, 80, 82, 103
Wrentham, 129
Wright, lieutenant, 22, 23
Wymondham, 60, 61, 62

Yarmouth, co. Norfolk, 12, 55, 67
Yates, Mr. of Norwich, 5, 6
York, 11, 87, 91, 98, 100
Yorkshire, 9, 83, 91, 103, 130

ERRATUM.—Page 51, *for* "died at Pembroke," *read* "died, as [William Herbert, earl of] Pembroke," &c.

J. B. Nichols and Sons, Printers, 25, Parliament Street.

www.ingramcontent.com/pod-product-compliance
Ingram Content Group UK Ltd.
Pitfield, Milton Keynes, MK11 3LW, UK
UKHW012340130625
459647UK00009B/421